MANY PATHS
to the
BAHÁ'Í FAITH

QUOTATIONS

A selection of passages from the
Bahá'í holy writings and other materials

Compiled by Nathan Thomas

Copyright © 2013 by Greysands Media, LLC

Cover design by Andrew Johnson

All rights reserved. This book or any portion thereof may not be reproduced or used in any manner whatsoever without the express written permission of the publisher.

First Printing, 2013
ISBN 978-1-939174-03-1

Greysands Media, LLC
www.greysandsmedia.com

THE WHYUNITE? SERIES BOOKS AND VIDEOS

MANY PATHS TO THE BAHÁ'Í FAITH
How people from different faith experiences discover fulfillment in the Bahá'í Faith

QUOTATIONS FOR MANY PATHS TO THE BAHÁ'Í FAITH
Selected passages from the Bahá'í holy writings and other materials

FIRESIDE TALK FOR MANY PATHS TO THE BAHÁ'Í FAITH
A video presentation about the Bahá'í Faith by the author, Nathan Thomas

MANIFEST YOUR POTENTIAL IN THE BAHÁ'Í FAITH
How the beliefs, practices, and vision of the Bahá'í Faith can change your life

QUOTATIONS FOR MANIFESTING YOUR POTENTIAL IN THE BAHÁ'Í FAITH
Selected passages from the Bahá'í holy writings and other materials

FIRESIDE TALK FOR MANIFESTING YOUR POTENTIAL IN THE BAHÁ'Í FAITH
A video presentation about the Bahá'í Faith by the author, Nathan Thomas

MAKING A BETTER WORLD WITH THE BAHÁ'Í FAITH
How Bahá'ís are transforming our world into a more unified, prosperous, and spiritual home for all mankind

QUOTATIONS FOR MAKING A BETTER WORLD WITH THE BAHÁ'Í FAITH
Selected passages from the Bahá'í holy writings and other materials

FIRESIDE TALK FOR MAKING A BETTER WORLD WITH THE BAHÁ'Í FAITH
A video presentation about the Bahá'í Faith by the author, Nathan Thomas

PATHS TO THE BAHÁ'Í FAITH
A nine-part collection of video interviews of Bahá'ís from a variety of backgrounds

Learn more at http://www.whyunite.com

TABLE OF CONTENTS

The WhyUnite? Series Books and Videos. iii
Table of Contents v
Preface to the WhyUnite? Series. vii

Introduction to Quotations for Many Paths to the Bahá'í Faith . . 9

Part I: Preparing for the Journey 1
   Chapter 1: Welcome to Many Paths: 3
   Chapter 2: What is the Bahá'í Faith? 11
   Chapter 3: Creating a Map for Many Paths. 21

Part II: The Paths 33
   Chapter 4: Paths from Judaism to the Bahá'í Faith 35
   Chapter 5: Paths from Christianity to the Bahá'í Faith 49
   Chapter 6: Paths from Islam to the Bahá'í Faith. 63
   Chapter 7: Paths from Hinduism to the Bahá'í Faith 83
   Chapter 8: Paths from Buddhism to the Bahá'í Faith 97
   Chapter 9: Paths from Native Religions to the Bahá'í Faith 109
   Chapter 10: Paths from Agnosticism to the Bahá'í Faith 125

Part III: Next Steps 145
   Chapter 11: Many Destinations for Many Paths 147
   Chapter 12: Conclusion 155

Appendix: Sources and Bibliography 165

PREFACE TO THE WHYUNITE? SERIES

A NEW WORLD RELIGION DEDICATED TO TRANSFORMING HUMANITY

The Bahá'í Faith is a world religion that brings teachings designed to help all of mankind while renewing the spiritual capacities of the human race. Founded by Bahá'u'lláh (meaning "the Glory of God" in Arabic) in the mid-nineteenth century, the goal of the Bahá'í Faith is to bring out the best in humanity. As Bahá'u'lláh wrote, through the teachings of this worldwide faith "every man will advance and develop until he attaineth the station at which he can manifest all the potential forces with which his inmost true self hath been endowed." (*Gleanings from the Writings of Bahá'u'lláh*, no. 27.5).

With practical teachings, a diverse global community, acceptance for of all the world's religions, and a message specifically designed to solve humanity's most pressing needs, the Bahá'í Faith brings a contemporary approach to religion that is unique among all the world's faiths. Bahá'u'lláh writes, "My object is none other than the betterment of the world and the tranquility of its peoples." (*Gleanings from the Writings of Bahá'u'lláh*, no. 131.2).

Today millions of people from every background have found this Faith through the individual investigation of truth. For them, it offers a compelling and fulfilling foundation for their spiritual experience. As 'Abdu'l-Bahá, the son and successor of Bahá'u'lláh said, "Man must walk in many paths and be subjected to various processes in his evolution upward." (*Promulgation of Universal Peace*, p. 295). Throughout all these paths we take in our lives, every person must judge for him or herself what is good and true for their own spiritual journey. For many, that process leads to the Bahá'í Faith.

AN INVITATION TO LEARN MORE WITH THE WHYUNITE? SERIES

The WhyUnite? Series is an individual initiative begun to produce compelling, unique, and practical content about the Bahá'í Faith. Our goal is to develop materials that educate, empower, and inspire people to follow their own path to the truth, to manifest their own potential as spiritual beings, and to make this world a better place in the process. To that end, we are dedicated to the continuous development of books, compilations, videos, and more to help people discover the spiritual richness, endless diversity, and wondrous wisdom offered to humanity through the Bahá'í Faith. Learn more about our work and get involved at www.whyunite.com.

INTRODUCTION TO QUOTATIONS FOR MANY PATHS TO THE BAHÁ'Í FAITH

10 ❷ Many Paths to the Bahá'í Faith: QUOTATIONS

This book is designed to be a companion to the book *Many Paths to the Bahá'í Faith,* which explores how people from every background are discovering a fulfilling, uplifting, and empowering spiritual journey to the Bahá'í Faith. It offers people from a wide variety of religious (and non-religious) backgrounds insight into why people are joining this new world religion. In the process the book provides a glimpse of the Bahá'í Faith, its teachings, practices, and theological foundations.

It covers:
- A basic introduction to the Bahá'í Faith
- How people prepare themselves for a spiritual journey
- Why people from Christian, Islamic, Jewish, Hindu, Buddhist, Native, and agnostic backgrounds become Bahá'ís
- What people of other faiths find in common with the Bahá'í teachings
- Challenges some people face in their journey to become Bahá'ís
- How becoming a Bahá'í offers hope, meaning, and purpose in life
- Suggested next steps for anyone investigating the Bahá'í Faith

ABOUT THE QUOTATIONS IN THIS BOOK

This book of quotations is intended to offer more direct insight into what the Bahá'í Faith directly says on the subjects covered in its companion book, *Many Paths to the Bahá'í Faith.* It includes many quotations from a wide variety of sources. Many of these sources are authentic documents written by the Founder of the Bahá'í Faith Himself, Bahá'u'lláh, which were often sealed with His personal seal. To that end, any quotations in this book attributed to Bahá'u'lláh are from approved translations of His works. It might be noted that Bahá'ís believe that Bahá'u'lláh revealed the Word of God for this age. Therefore His works are very important to the Bahá'í community. Any reader of His words, though, will soon notice that He revealed His works in many styles. At some times He revealed them as a "lawgiver," at other times He revealed them as a "mystic" or spiritual guide, and at other times as a counselor to His followers. He even revealed works in the voice of God Himself. The reality is, for many people, reading the words of Bahá'u'lláh can take some getting used to. But once people get used to the different tone and language of the Holy Writings, many spend their entire lives exploring the endless meanings and implications of the words revealed by the Founder of this faith.

In addition this book includes many quotations from Bahá'u'lláh's son and successor, 'Abdu'l-Bahá. While 'Abdu'l-Bahá did write many books and letters that can be considered authentic, he also gave many talks throughout his long career as a Central Figure of this Faith. The reader should realize, therefore, that many of the quotations that were gathered from such lectures and forums were written down by observers. Thus some of these passages are not considered authoritative, but can be used for personal edification and spiritual discovery. To that end, the reader should recognize that some of the materials from such works should be balanced with everything else in the Bahá'í Writings that is considered authoritative.

After the Writings of Bahá'u'lláh and 'Abdu'l-Bahá, this book also includes quotations from the grandson of 'Abdu'l-Bahá, the appointed Guardian of the Bahá'í Faith, Shoghi Effendi. These writings include materials, letters, and books that the Guardian wrote to the Bahá'í world, and to individual believers. Sometimes he wrote these letters himself, in other cases they were recorded by his secretaries. The Guardian's writings are considered an authoritative source for guidance and interpretation of the Word of God. And while this material is considered a critical source for understanding the teachings, concepts, and ideas of the Bahá'í Faith, they must also be approached with care when taken from letters to individuals. That is, in some cases direction may have been given to one person that would not necessarily fit the whole of humanity. Therefore, again, Bahá'ís are encouraged to weigh and judge for themselves in these matters with respect to all the other authoritative content we have available to us.

In addition, this book includes writings of the Universal House of Justice, the authoritative word of the supreme governing body of the worldwide Bahá'í community. It also includes works from other sources such as the Bahá'í International Community, which is an agency of the Universal House of Justice that works with non-governmental organizations around the world. These works, while not authoritative, shed insight into the inner workings of the Faith and offer a global perspective on how things should be carried out in the Bahá'í world and beyond.

SUGGESTIONS FOR READING THE QUOTATIONS

It is strongly suggested that the reader explore the book that inspired this collection of quotations, *Many Paths to the Bahá'í Faith*, before diving fully into the quotes in this book. The fact is, the Bahá'í Faith is rich and nuanced. Many of these quotations are better understood when their context and perspective is considered. In addition, it can also be helpful to read and study these books in book clubs or study classes with other people, including and especially other Bahá'ís. It can be very useful to explore spiritual topics with others, to hear their ideas, their interpretations, and their questions and concerns when one is making his or her own decisions in spiritual development.

Lastly, it is encouraged that new believers take their time when it comes to studying the Bahá'í Writings. This is because it takes patience for many to learn the language of these works, to gain confidence with the terms, to acquire a taste for the grammatical and stylistic approaches, and to build up a solid foundation of understanding that can then be used as a lens to discover, interpret, and cultivate spiritual truths in our lives.

14 ❓ Many Paths to the Bahá'í Faith: QUOTATIONS

PART I: PREPARING FOR THE JOURNEY

CHAPTER 1:

WELCOME TO MANY PATHS

4 ❓ Many Paths to the Bahá'í Faith: QUOTATIONS

FROM THE WRITINGS OF BAHÁ'U'LLÁH

1.1 THE VALLEY OF SEARCH... The steed of this Valley is patience; without patience the wayfarer on this journey will reach nowhere and attain no goal. Nor should he ever be downhearted; if he strive for a hundred thousand years and yet fail to behold the beauty of the Friend, he should not falter.

1.2 Only when the lamp of search, of earnest striving, of longing desire, of passionate devotion, of fervid love, of rapture, and ecstasy, is kindled within the seeker's heart, and the breeze of His loving-kindness is wafted upon his soul, will the darkness of error be dispelled, the mists of doubts and misgivings be dissipated, and the lights of knowledge and certitude envelop his being. At that hour will the mystic Herald, bearing the joyful tidings of the Spirit, shine forth from the City of God resplendent as the morn, and, through the trumpet-blast of knowledge, will awaken the heart, the soul, and the spirit from the slumber of negligence. Then will the manifold favours and outpouring grace of the holy and everlasting Spirit confer such new life upon the seeker that he will find himself endowed with a new eye, a new ear, a new heart, and a new mind. He will contemplate the manifest signs of the universe, and will penetrate the hidden mysteries of the soul. Gazing with the eye of God, he will perceive within every atom a door that leadeth him to the stations of absolute certitude. He will discover in all things the mysteries of divine Revelation and the evidences of an everlasting manifestation.

1.3 Whoso hath searched the depths of the oceans that lie hid within these exalted words, and fathomed their import, can be said to have discovered a glimmer of the unspeakable glory with which this mighty, this sublime, and most holy Revelation hath been endowed.

1.4 Hear Me, ye mortal birds! In the Rose Garden of changeless splendor a Flower hath begun to bloom, compared to which every other flower is but a thorn, and before the brightness of Whose glory the very essence of beauty must pale and wither. Arise, therefore, and, with the whole enthusiasm of your hearts, with all the eagerness of your souls, the full fervor of your will, and the concentrated efforts of your entire being, strive to attain the paradise of His presence, and endeavor to inhale the fragrance of the incorruptible Flower, to breathe the sweet savors of holiness, and to obtain a portion of this perfume of celestial glory. Whoso followeth this counsel will break his chains asunder, will taste the abandonment of enraptured love, will attain unto his heart's desire, and will surrender his soul into the hands of his Beloved. Bursting through his cage, he will, even as the bird of the spirit, wing his flight to his holy and everlasting nest.

FROM THE WRITINGS AND UTTERANCES OF 'ABDU'L-BAHÁ

1.5   When, however, thou dost contemplate the innermost essence of all things, and the individuality of each, thou wilt behold the signs of thy Lord's mercy in every created thing, and see the spreading rays of His Names and Attributes throughout all the realm of being, with evidences which none will deny save the froward and the unaware. Then wilt thou observe that the universe is a scroll that discloseth His hidden secrets, which are preserved in the well-guarded Tablet. And not an atom of all the atoms in existence, not a creature from amongst the creatures but speaketh His praise and telleth of His attributes and names, revealeth the glory of His might and guideth to His oneness and His mercy: and none will gainsay this who hath ears to hear, eyes to see, and a mind that is sound.

1.6   O Thou, my God, Who guidest the seeker to the pathway that leadeth aright, Who deliverest the lost and blinded soul out of the wastes of perdition, Thou Who bestowest upon the sincere great bounties and favours, Who guardest the frightened within Thine impregnable refuge, Who answerest, from Thine all-highest horizon, the cry of those who cry out unto Thee. Praised be Thou, O my Lord! Thou hast guided the distracted out of the death of unbelief, and hast brought those who draw nigh unto Thee to the journey's goal, and hast rejoiced the assured among Thy servants by granting them their most cherished desires, and hast, from Thy Kingdom of beauty, opened before the faces of those who yearn after Thee the gates of reunion, and hast rescued them from the fires of deprivation and loss—so that they hastened unto Thee and gained Thy presence, and arrived at Thy welcoming door, and received of gifts an abundant share.

O my Lord, they thirsted, Thou didst lift to their parched lips the waters of reunion. O Tender One, Bestowing One, Thou didst calm their pain with the balm of Thy bounty and grace, and didst heal their ailments with the sovereign medicine of Thy compassion. O Lord, make firm their feet on Thy straight path, make wide for them the needle's eye, and cause them, dressed in royal robes, to walk in glory for ever and ever.

Verily art Thou the Generous, the Ever-Giving, the Precious, the Most Bountiful. There is none other God but Thee, the Mighty, the Powerful, the Exalted, the Victorious.

1.7 I beg of God to open before thine eyes the gates of discoveries and perceptions, that thou mayest become informed of His mysteries in this most manifest of days.

1.8 Thou didst ask as to acquiring knowledge: read thou the Books and Tablets of God, and the articles written to demonstrate the truth of this Faith. Included among them are the Íqán, which hath been translated into English, the works of Mirza Abu'l-Fadl, and those of some others among the believers. In the days to come a great number of holy Tablets and other sacred writings will be translated, and thou shouldst read these as well. Likewise, ask thou of God that the magnet of His love should draw unto thee the knowledge of Him. Once a soul becometh holy in all things, purified, sanctified, the gates of the knowledge of God will open wide before his eyes.

1.9 Verily in this are signs for those who have eyes to see.

1.10 Some think that the body is the substance and exists by itself, and that the spirit is accidental and depends upon the substance of the body, although, on the contrary, the rational soul is the substance, and the body depends upon it. If the accident—that is to say, the body—be destroyed, the substance, the spirit, remains.

Second, the rational soul, meaning the human spirit, does not descend into the body—that is to say, it does not enter it, for descent and entrance are characteristics of bodies, and the rational soul is exempt from this. The spirit never entered this body, so in quitting it, it will not be in need of an abiding-place: no, the spirit is connected with the body, as this light is with this mirror. When the mirror is clear and perfect, the light of the lamp will be apparent in it, and when the mirror becomes covered with dust or breaks, the light will disappear.

The rational soul—that is to say, the human spirit—has neither entered this body nor existed through it; so after the disintegration of the composition of the body, how should it be in need of a substance through which it may exist? On the contrary, the rational soul is the substance through which the body exists. The personality of the rational soul is from its beginning; it is not due to the instrumentality of the body, but the state and the personality of the rational soul may be strengthened in this world; it will make progress and will attain to the degrees of perfection, or it will remain in the lowest abyss of ignorance, veiled and deprived from beholding the signs of God.

FROM THE WRITINGS AND LETTERS WRITTEN BY, OR ON BEHALF OF, SHOGHI EFFENDI

1.11 The Faith standing identified with the name of Bahá'u'lláh disclaims any intention to belittle any of the Prophets gone before Him, to whittle down any of their teachings, to obscure, however slightly, the radiance of their Revelations, to oust them from the hearts of their followers, to abrogate the fundamentals of their doctrines, to discard any of their revealed Books, or to suppress the legitimate aspirations of their adherents. Repudiating the claim of any religion to be the final revelation of God to man, disclaiming finality for His own Revelation, Bahá'u'lláh inculcates the basic principle of the relativity of religious truth, the continuity of Divine Revelation, the progressiveness of religious experience. His aim is to widen the basis of all revealed religions and to unravel the mysteries of their scriptures. He insists on the unqualified recognition of the unity of their purpose, restates the eternal verities they enshrine, coordinates their functions, distinguishes the essential and the authentic from the nonessential and spurious in their teachings, separates the God-given truths from the priest-prompted superstitions, and on this as a basis proclaims the possibility, and even prophecies the inevitability, of their unification, and the consummation of their highest hopes.

1.12   As we almost never attain any spiritual goal without seeing the next goal we must attain still beyond our reach, he urges you, who, have come so far already on the path of spirituality, not to fret about the distance you still have to cover! It is an indefinite journey, and, no doubt in the next world the soul is privileged to draw closer to God than is possible when bound on this physical plane.

CHAPTER 2:

WHAT IS THE BAHÁ'Í FAITH?

FROM THE WRITINGS OF BAHÁ'U'LLÁH

2.1   Great indeed is this Day! The allusions made to it in all the sacred Scriptures as the Day of God attest its greatness. The soul of every Prophet of God, of every Divine Messenger, hath thirsted for this wondrous Day. All the diverse kindreds of the earth have, likewise, yearned to attain it. No sooner, however, had the Day Star of His Revelation manifested itself in the heaven of God's Will, than all, except those whom the Almighty was pleased to guide, were found dumbfounded and heedless.

2.2   We desire but the good of the world and the happiness of the nations; yet they deem Us a stirrer up of strife and sedition worthy of bondage and banishment.... That all nations should become one in faith and all men as brothers; that the bonds of affection and unity between the sons of men should be strengthened; that diversity of religion should cease, and differences of race be annulled—what harm is there in this?... Yet so it shall be; these fruitless strifes, these ruinous wars shall pass away, and the 'Most Great Peace' shall come.... Yet do We see your kings and rulers lavishing their treasures more freely on means for the destruction of the human race than on that which would conduce to the happiness of mankind.... These strifes and this bloodshed and discord must cease, and all men be as one kindred and one family.... Let not a man glory in this, that he loves his country; let him rather glory in this, that he loves his kind...

2.3   We, verily, have come to unite and weld together all that dwell on earth.

2.4   Give ear unto the verses of God which He Who is the sacred Lote-Tree reciteth unto you. They are assuredly the infallible balance, established by God, the Lord of this world and the next. Through them the soul of man is caused to wing its flight towards the Dayspring of Revelation, and the heart of every true believer is suffused with light. Such are the laws which God hath enjoined upon you, such His commandments prescribed unto you in His Holy Tablet; obey them with joy and gladness, for this is best for you, did ye but know.

2.5   I was but a man like others, asleep upon My couch, when lo, the breezes of the All-Glorious were wafted over Me, and taught Me the knowledge of all that hath been. This thing is not from Me, but from One Who is Almighty and All-Knowing. And He bade Me lift up My voice between earth and heaven, and for this there befell Me what hath caused the tears of every man of understanding to flow. The learning current amongst men I studied not; their schools I entered not. Ask of the city wherein I dwelt, that thou mayest be well assured that I am not of them who speak falsely. This is but a leaf which the winds of the will of thy Lord, the Almighty, the All-Praised, have stirred. Can it be still when the tempestuous winds are blowing? Nay, by Him Who is the Lord of all Names and Attributes! They move it as they list. The evanescent is as nothing before Him Who is the Ever-Abiding. His all-compelling summons hath reached Me, and caused Me to speak His praise amidst all people. I was indeed as one dead when His behest was uttered. The hand of the will of thy Lord, the Compassionate, the Merciful, transformed Me.

2.6   While engulfed in tribulations I heard a most wondrous, a most sweet voice, calling above My head. Turning My face, I beheld a Maiden—the embodiment of the remembrance of the name of My Lord—suspended in the air before Me. So rejoiced was she in her very soul that her countenance shone with the ornament of the good pleasure of God, and her cheeks glowed with the brightness of the All-Merciful. Betwixt earth and heaven she was raising a call which captivated the hearts and minds of men. She was imparting to both My inward and outer being tidings which rejoiced My soul, and the souls of God's honoured servants.

　　　　Pointing with her finger unto My head, she addressed all who are in heaven and all who are on earth, saying: By God! This is the Best-Beloved of the worlds, and yet ye comprehend not. This is the Beauty of God amongst you, and the power of His sovereignty within you, could ye but understand. This is the Mystery of God and His Treasure, the Cause of God and His glory unto all who are in the kingdoms of Revelation and of creation, if ye be of them that perceive. This is He Whose

Presence is the ardent desire of the denizens of the Realm of eternity, and of them that dwell within the Tabernacle of glory, and yet from His Beauty do ye turn aside.

FROM THE WRITINGS AND UTTERANCES OF 'ABDU'L-BAHÁ

2.7   When delivering the glad tidings, speak out and say: the Promised One of all the world's peoples hath now been made manifest. For each and every people, and every religion, await a Promised One, and Bahá'u'lláh is that One Who is awaited by all; and therefore the Cause of Bahá'u'lláh will bring about the oneness of mankind, and the tabernacle of unity will be upraised on the heights of the world, and the banners of the universality of all humankind will be unfurled on the peaks of the earth. When thou dost loose thy tongue to deliver this great good news, this will become the means of teaching the people.

2.8   Unless these Teachings are effectively spread among the people, until the old ways, the old concepts, are gone and forgotten, this world of being will find no peace, nor will it reflect the perfections of the Heavenly Kingdom. Strive ye with all your hearts to make the heedless conscious, to waken those who sleep, to bring knowledge to the ignorant, to make the blind to see, the deaf to hear, and restore the dead to life.

2.9   Throughout the world generally war and dissension prevailed. At this time Bahá'u'lláh appeared in Persia and began devoting Himself to the uplift and education of the people. He united divergent sects and creeds, removed religious, racial, patriotic and political prejudices and established a strong bond of unity and reconciliation among varying degrees and classes of mankind. The enmity then existing among the people was so bitter and intense that even ordinary association was out of the question. They would not meet and consult with each other at all. Through the power of the teachings of Bahá'u'lláh the most wonderful results were witnessed. He removed the prejudices and hatred from human hearts and wrought such transformation in their attitudes toward each other that today in Persia there is perfect accord among hitherto bigoted religionists, varying sects and divergent classes. This was not an easy accomplishment, for Bahá'u'lláh underwent severe trials, great difficulties and violent persecution. He was imprisoned, tortures were inflicted upon Him, and finally He was banished from His native land. He bore every ordeal and infliction cheerfully. In His successive exiles from country to country up to the time of His ascension from this world, He was enabled to promulgate His teachings, even from prison. Wherever His oppressors sent Him, He hoisted the standard of the oneness of the world of humanity and promulgated the principles of the unity of mankind. Some of these principles are as follows. First, it is incumbent upon all mankind to investigate truth. If such investigation be made, all should agree and be united, for truth or reality is not multiple; it is not divisible. The different religions have one truth underlying them; therefore, their reality is one.

2.10 From time immemorial the divine teachings have been successively revealed, and the bounties of the Holy Spirit have ever been emanating. All the teachings are one reality, for reality is single and does not admit multiplicity. Therefore, the divine Prophets are one, inasmuch as They reveal the one reality, the Word of God. Abraham announced teachings founded upon reality, Moses proclaimed reality, Christ established reality and Bahá'u'lláh was the Messenger and Herald of reality. But humanity, having forsaken the one essential and fundamental reality which underlies the religion of God, and holding blindly to imitations of ancestral forms and interpretations of belief, is separated and divided in the strife, contention and bigotry of various sects and religious factions. If all should be true to the original reality of the Prophet and His teaching, the peoples and nations of the world would become unified, and these differences which cause separation would be lost sight of. To accomplish this great and needful unity in reality, Bahá'u'lláh appeared in the Orient and renewed the foundations of the divine teachings. His revelation of the Word embodies completely the teachings of all the Prophets, expressed in principles and precepts applicable to the needs and conditions of the modern world, amplified and adapted to present-day questions and critical human problems. That is to say, the words of Bahá'u'lláh are the essences of the words of the Prophets of the past. They are the very spirit of the age and the cause of the unity and illumination of the East and the West. The followers of His teachings are in conformity with the precepts and commands of all the former heavenly Messengers. Differences and dissensions, which destroy the foundations of the world of humanity and are contrary to the will and good pleasure of God, disappear completely in the light of the revelation of Bahá'u'lláh; difficult problems are solved, unity and love are established. For the good pleasure of God is the effulgence of love and the establishment of unity and fellowship in the human world, whereas discord, contention, warfare and strife are satanic outcomes and contrary to the will of the Merciful. In order that human souls, minds and spirits may attain advancement, tranquillity and vision in broader horizons of unity and knowledge, Bahá'u'lláh proclaimed certain principles or teachings, some of which I will mention.

2.11 Briefly, the Blessed Perfection bore all these ordeals and calamities in order that our hearts might become enkindled and radiant, our spirits be glorified, our faults become virtues, our ignorance be transformed into knowledge; in order that we might attain the real fruits of humanity and acquire heavenly graces; in order that, although pilgrims upon earth, we should travel the road of the heavenly Kingdom, and, although needy and poor, we might receive the treasures of eternal life. For this has He borne these difficulties and sorrows.

FROM THE WRITINGS AND LETTERS WRITTEN BY, OR ON BEHALF OF, SHOGHI EFFENDI

2.12 The Bahá'í Faith upholds the unity of God, recognizes the unity of His Prophets, and inculcates the principle of the oneness and wholeness of the entire human race. it proclaims the necessity and the inevitability of the unification of mankind, asserts that it is gradually approaching, and claims that nothing short of the transmuting spirit of God, working through His chosen Mouthpiece in this day, can ultimately succeed in bringing it about. It, moreover, enjoins upon its followers the primary duty of an unfettered search after truth, condemns all manner of prejudice and superstition, declares the purpose of religion to be the promotion of amity and concord, proclaims its essential harmony with science, and recognizes it as the foremost agency for the pacification and the orderly progress of human society. It unequivocally maintains the principle of equal rights, opportunities and privileges for men and women, insists on compulsory education, eliminates extremes of poverty and wealth, abolishes the institution of priesthood, prohibits slavery, asceticism, mendicancy and monasticism, prescribes monogamy, discourages divorce, emphasizes the necessity of strict obedience to one's government, exalts any work performed in the spirit of service to the level of worship, urges either the creation or selection of an auxiliary international language, and delineates the outlines of those institutions that must establish and perpetuate the general peace of mankind.

2.13　The independent search after truth, unfettered by superstition or tradition; the oneness of the entire human race, the pivotal principle and fundamental doctrine of the Faith; the basic unity of all religions; the condemnation of all forms of prejudice, whether religious, racial, class or national; the harmony which must exist between religion and science; the equality of men and women, the two wings on which the bird of human kind is able to soar; the introduction of compulsory education; the adoption of a universal auxiliary language; the abolition of the extremes of wealth and poverty; the institution of a world tribunal for the adjudication of disputes between nations; the exaltation of work, performed in the spirit of service, to the rank of worship; the glorification of justice as the ruling principle in human society, and of religion as a bulwark for the protection of all peoples and nations; and the establishment of a permanent and universal peace as the supreme goal of all mankind—these stand out as the essential elements of that Divine polity which He proclaimed to leaders of public thought as well as to the masses at large in the course of these missionary journeys.

FROM THE WRITINGS AND LETTERS WRITTEN BY, OR ON BEHALF OF, THE UNIVERSAL HOUSE OF JUSTICE

2.14 The Bahá'í Faith regards the current world confusion and calamitous condition in human affairs as a natural phase in an organic process leading ultimately and irresistibly to the unification of the human race in a single social order whose boundaries are those of the planet. The human race, as a distinct, organic unit, has passed through evolutionary stages analogous to the stages of infancy and childhood in the lives of its individual members, and is now in the culminating period of its turbulent adolescence approaching its long-awaited coming of age.

2.15 ...Whatever suffering and turmoil the years immediately ahead may hold, however dark the immediate circumstances, the Bahá'í community believes that humanity can confront this supreme trial with confidence in its ultimate outcome. Far from signaling the end of civilization, the convulsive changes towards which humanity is being ever more rapidly impelled will serve to release the "potentialities inherent in the station of man" and reveal "the full measure of his destiny on earth, the innate excellence of his reality".

CHAPTER 3:
CREATING A MAP FOR MANY PATHS

FROM THE WRITINGS OF BAHÁ'U'LLÁH

3.1 By the righteousness of God! These are the days in which God hath proved the hearts of the entire company of His Messengers and Prophets, and beyond them those that stand guard over His sacred and inviolable Sanctuary, the inmates of the celestial Pavilion and dwellers of the Tabernacle of Glory. How severe, therefore, the test to which they who join partners with God must needs be subjected!

3.2 Consider the past. How many, both high and low, have, at all times, yearningly awaited the advent of the Manifestations of God in the sanctified persons of His chosen Ones. How often have they expected His coming, how frequently have they prayed that the breeze of Divine mercy might blow, and the promised Beauty step forth from behind the veil of concealment, and be made manifest to all the world. And whensoever the portals of grace did open, and the clouds of divine bounty did rain upon mankind, and the light of the Unseen did shine above the horizon of celestial might, they all denied Him, and turned away from His face—the face of God Himself....

3.3 Reflect, what could have been the motive for such deeds? What could have prompted such behavior towards the Revealers of the beauty of the All-Glorious? Whatever in days gone by hath been the cause of the denial and opposition of those people hath now led to the perversity of the people of this age. To maintain that the testimony of Providence was incomplete, that it hath therefore been the cause of the denial of the people, is but open blasphemy. How far from the grace of the All-Bountiful and from His loving providence and tender mercies it is to single out a soul from amongst all men for the guidance of His creatures, and, on one hand, to withhold from Him the full measure of His divine testimony, and, on the other, inflict severe retribution on His people for having turned away from His chosen One! Nay, the manifold bounties of the Lord of all beings have, at all times, through the Manifestations of His Divine Essence, encompassed the earth and all that dwell therein. Not for a moment hath His grace been withheld, nor have the showers of His loving-kindness ceased to rain upon mankind. Consequently, such behavior can be attributed to naught save the petty-mindedness of such souls as tread the valley of arrogance and pride, are lost in the wilds of remoteness, walk in the ways of their idle fancy, and follow the dictates of the leaders of their faith. Their chief concern is mere opposition; their sole desire is to ignore the truth. Unto every discerning observer it is evident and manifest that had these people in the days of each of the Manifestations of the Sun of Truth sanctified their eyes, their ears, and their hearts from whatever they had seen, heard, and felt, they surely would not have been deprived of beholding the beauty of God, nor strayed far from the habitations of glory. But having weighed the testimony of God by the standard of their own knowledge, gleaned from the teachings of the leaders of their faith, and found it at variance with their limited understanding, they arose to perpetrate such unseemly acts....

3.4 It behoveth them to choose as the best provision for their journey reliance upon God, and to clothe themselves with the love of their Lord, the Most Exalted, the All-Glorious. If they do so, their words shall influence their hearers.

3.5 Sanctify your souls from whatsoever is not of God, and taste ye the sweetness of rest within the pale of His vast and mighty Revelation, and beneath the shadow of His supreme and infallible authority. Suffer not yourselves to be wrapt in the dense veils of your selfish desires, inasmuch as I have perfected in every one of you My creation, so that the excellence of My handiwork may be fully revealed unto men.

3.6 O My brother! When a true seeker determineth to take the step of search in the path leading unto the knowledge of the Ancient of Days, he must, before all else, cleanse his heart, which is the seat of the revelation of the inner mysteries of God, from the obscuring dust of all acquired knowledge, and the allusions of the embodiments of satanic fancy. He must purge his breast, which is the sanctuary of the abiding love of the Beloved, of every defilement, and sanctify his soul from all that pertaineth to water and clay, from all shadowy and ephemeral attachments. He must so cleanse his heart that no remnant of either love or hate may linger therein, lest that love blindly incline him to

Chapter 3: Creating a Map for Many Paths 25

error, or that hate repel him away from the truth. Even as thou dost witness in this Day how most of the people, because of such love and hate, are bereft of the immortal Face, have strayed far from the Embodiments of the Divine mysteries, and, shepherdless, are roaming through the wilderness of oblivion and error.

3.7   The stages that mark the wayfarer's journey from the abode of dust to the heavenly homeland are said to be seven. Some have called these Seven Valleys, and others, Seven Cities. And they say that until the wayfarer taketh leave of self, and traverseth these stages, he shall never reach to the ocean of nearness and union, nor drink of the peerless wine.

3.8   These journeys have no visible ending in the world of time, but the severed wayfarer—if invisible confirmation descend upon him and the Guardian of the Cause assist him—may cross these seven stages in seven steps, nay rather in seven breaths, nay rather in a single breath, if God will and desire it.

3.9   On this journey the traveler abideth in every land and dwelleth in every region. In every face, he seeketh the beauty of the Friend; in every country he looketh for the Beloved. He joineth every company, and seeketh fellowship with every soul, that haply in some mind he may uncover the secret of the Friend, or in some face he may behold the beauty of the Loved One.

3.10 O My Brother, journey upon these planes in the spirit of search, not in blind imitation.

FROM THE WRITINGS AND UTTERANCES OF 'ABDU'L-BAHÁ

3.11 Man must walk in many paths and be subjected to various processes in his evolution upward. Physically he is not born in full stature but passes through consecutive stages of fetus, infant, childhood, youth, maturity and old age. Suppose he had the power to remain young throughout his life. He then would not understand the meaning of old age and could not believe it existed. If he could not realize the condition of old age, he would not know that he was young. He would not know the difference between young and old without experiencing the old. Unless you have passed through the state of infancy, how would you know this was an infant beside you? If there were no wrong, how would you recognize the right? If it were not for sin, how would you appreciate virtue? If evil deeds were unknown, how could you commend good actions? If sickness did not exist, how would you understand health? Evil is nonexistent; it is the absence of good. Sickness is the loss of health; poverty, the lack of riches. When wealth disappears, you are poor; you look within the treasure box but find nothing there. Without knowledge there is ignorance; therefore, ignorance is simply the lack of knowledge. Death is the absence of life. Therefore, on the one hand, we have existence; on the other, nonexistence, negation or absence of existence.

3.12 Briefly, the journey of the soul is necessary. The pathway of life is the road which leads to divine knowledge and attainment. Without training and guidance the soul could never progress beyond the conditions of its lower nature, which is ignorant and defective

3.13 Furthermore, this immortal human soul is endowed with two means of perception: One is effected through instrumentality; the other, independently. For instance, the soul sees through the instrumentality of the eye, hears with the ear, smells through the nostrils and grasps objects with the hands. These are the actions or operations of the soul through instruments. But in the world of dreams the soul sees when the eyes are closed. The man is seemingly dead, lies there as dead; the ears do not hear, yet he hears. The body lies there, but he—that is, the soul—travels, sees, observes. All the instruments of the body are inactive, all the functions seemingly useless. Notwithstanding this, there is an immediate and vivid perception by the soul. Exhilaration is experienced. The soul journeys, perceives, senses. It often happens that a man in a state of wakefulness has not been able to accomplish the solution of a problem, and when he goes to sleep, he will reach that solution in a dream. How often it has happened that he has dreamed, even as the prophets have dreamed, of the future; and events which have thus been foreshadowed have come to pass literally.

3.14 The first teaching of Bahá'u'lláh is the duty incumbent upon all to investigate reality. What does it mean to investigate reality? It means that man must forget all hearsay and examine truth himself, for he does not know whether statements he hears are in accordance with reality or not. Wherever he finds truth or reality, he must hold to it, forsaking, discarding all else; for outside of reality there is naught but superstition and imagination. For example, during the days of Jesus Christ the Jews were expecting the appearance of the Messiah, praying and beseeching God day and night that the Promised One might appear. Why did they reject Him when He did appear? They denied Him absolutely, refused to believe in Him. There was no abuse and persecution which they did not heap upon Him. They reviled Him with curses, placed a crown of thorns upon His head, led Him through the streets in scorn and derision and finally crucified Him. Why did they do this? Because they did not investigate the truth or reality of Christ and were not able to recognize Him as the Messiah of God. Had they investigated sincerely for themselves, they would surely have believed in Him, respected Him and bowed before Him in reverence. They would have considered His manifestation the greatest bestowal upon mankind. They would have accepted Him as the very Savior of man; but, alas, they were veiled, they held to imitations of ancestral beliefs and hearsay and did not investigate the truth of Christ. They were submerged in the sea of superstitions and were, therefore, deprived of witnessing that glorious bounty; they were withheld from the fragrances or breaths of the Holy Spirit and suffered in themselves the greatest debasement and degradation.

3.15 Thus there have been many holy Manifestations of God. One thousand years ago, two hundred thousand years ago, one million years ago, the bounty of God was flowing, the radiance of God was shining, the dominion of God was existing.

3.16 It is, therefore, clear that in order to make any progress in the search after truth we must relinquish superstition. If all seekers would follow this principle they would obtain a clear vision of the truth.

If five people meet together to seek for truth, they must begin by cutting themselves free from all their own special conditions and renouncing all preconceived ideas. In order to find truth we must give up our prejudices, our own small trivial notions; an open receptive mind is essential. If our chalice is full of self, there is no room in it for the water of life. The fact that we imagine ourselves to be right and everybody else wrong is the greatest of all obstacles in the path towards unity, and unity is necessary if we would reach truth, for truth is one.

Therefore it is imperative that we should renounce our own particular prejudices and superstitions if we earnestly desire to seek the truth. Unless we make a distinction in our minds between dogma, superstition and prejudice on the one hand, and truth on the other, we cannot succeed. When we are in earnest in our search for anything we look for it everywhere. This principle we must carry out in our search for truth.

FROM THE WRITINGS AND LETTERS WRITTEN BY, OR ON BEHALF OF, SHOGHI EFFENDI

3.17 The Bahá'í Faith upholds the unity of God, recognizes the unity of His Prophets, and inculcates the principle of the oneness and wholeness of the entire human race. It proclaims the necessity and the inevitability of the unification of mankind, asserts that it is gradually approaching, and claims that nothing short of the transmuting spirit of God, working through His chosen Mouthpiece in this day, can ultimately succeed in bringing it about. It, moreover, enjoins upon its followers the primary duty of an unfettered search after truth, condemns all manner of prejudice and superstition, declares the purpose of religion to be the promotion of amity and concord, proclaims its essential harmony with science, and recognizes it as the foremost agency for the pacification and the orderly progress of human society...

3.18 Between the truth which comes from God through His Prophets, and the glimmerings, often misunderstood and misinterpreted, of truth which come from the philosophers and thinkers, there is an immense difference. We must never, under any circumstances, confuse the two.

Bahá'u'lláh has said that learning can be the veil between the soul of man and the eternal truth; in other words, between man and the knowledge of God. We have seen that many people who become very advanced in the study of modern physical sciences are led to deny God, and to deny His Prophets. That does not mean that God and the Prophets have not existed and do not exist. It only means that knowledge has become a veil between their hearts and the light of God.

3.19 Regarding the questions you asked: Self has really two meanings, or is used in two senses, in the Bahá'í writings; one is self, the identity of the individual created by God. This is the self mentioned in such passages as 'he hath known God who hath known himself etc.'. The other self is the ego, the dark, animalistic heritage each one of us has, the lower nature that can develop into a monster of selfishness, brutality, lust and so on. It is this self we must struggle against, or this side of our natures, in order to strengthen and free the spirit within us and help it to attain perfection.

Self-sacrifice means to subordinate this lower nature and its desires to the more godly and noble side of ourselves. Ultimately, in its highest sense, self-sacrifice means to give our will and our all to God to do with as He pleases. Then He purifies and glorifies our true self until it becomes a shining and wonderful reality.

3.20 Our past is not the thing that matters so much in this world as what we intend to do with our future. The inestimable value of religion is that when a man is vitally connected with it, through a real and living belief in it and in the Prophet Who brought it, he receives a strength greater than his own which helps him to develop his good characteristics and overcome his bad ones. The whole purpose of religion is to change not only our thoughts but our acts; when we believe in God and His Prophet and His Teachings, we are growing, even though we perhaps thought ourselves incapable of growth and change!

FROM THE WRITINGS AND LETTERS WRITTEN BY, OR ON BEHALF OF, THE UNIVERSAL HOUSE OF JUSTICE

3.21 It has been suggested that the words of Bahá'u'lláh that a true seeker should "so cleanse his heart that no remnant of either love or hate may linger therein, lest that love blindly incline him to error, or that hate repel him away from the truth," support the viewpoint of methodological agnosticism. But we believe that on deeper reflection it will be recognized that love and hate are emotional attachments or repulsions that can irrationally influence the seeker; they are not aspects of the truth itself. Moreover, the whole passage concerns taking "the step of search in the path leading to the knowledge of the Ancient of Days" and is summarized by Bahá'u'lláh in the words: "Our purpose in revealing these convincing and weighty utterances is to impress upon the seeker that he should regard all else beside God as transient, and count all things save Him, Who is the Object of all adoration, as utter nothingness." It is in this context that He says, near the beginning of the passage, that the seeker must, "before all else, cleanse and purify his heart ... from the obscuring dust of all acquired knowledge, and the allusions of the embodiments of satanic fancy." It is similar, we think, to Bahá'u'lláh's injunction to look upon the Manifestation with His Own eyes. In scientific investigation when searching after the facts of any matter a Bahá'í must, of course, be entirely open-minded, but in his interpretation of the facts and his evaluation of evidence we do not see by what logic he can ignore the truth of the Bahá'í Revelation which he has already accepted; to do so would, we feel, be both hypocritical and unscholarly.

3.22 The sundering of science and religion is but one example of the tendency of the human mind (which is necessarily limited in its capacity) to concentrate on one virtue, one aspect of truth, one goal, to the exclusion of others. This leads, in extreme cases, to fanaticism and the utter distortion of truth, and in all cases to some degree of imbalance and inaccuracy. A scholar who is imbued with an understanding of the broad teachings of the Faith will always remember that being a scholar does not exempt him from the primal duties and purposes for which all human beings are created. All men, not scholars alone, are exhorted to seek out and uphold the truth, no matter how uncomfortable it may be. But they are also exhorted to be wise in their utterance, to be tolerant of the views of others, to be courteous in their behaviour and speech, not to sow the seeds of doubt in faithful hearts, to look at the good rather than at the bad, to avoid conflict and contention, to be reverent, to be faithful to the Covenant of God, to promote His Faith and safeguard its honour, and to educate their fellowmen, giving milk to babes and meat to those who are stronger.

3.23 In freeing the believers from the religious rituals of the past and from those customs which are contrary to the Bahá'í principles, the institutions of the Faith should be careful not to press the friends to arbitrarily discard those local tradition which are harmless and often colourful characteristic of particular peoples and tribes.

OTHER SOURCES

3.24 The study of the history and culture, if based on the premise of the oneness of humanity, should lead to a growing appreciation of the diverse religious traditions. This appreciation will be strengthened by interaction with people of different faiths, if the purpose is to promote unity. An everyday familiarity with people of different backgrounds will help each individual to lift the veil of cultural difference and see beneath it the shared humanity of all the peoples of the world. "O people! consort with the followers of all religions in a spirit of friendliness and fellowship," Bahá'u'lláh commands His followers. "Consorting with people hath promoted and will continue to promote unity and concord". (Bahá'í International Community, 1995 Jan 10, *Promoting Religious Tolerance*)

3.25 While believing, as part of our faith, that all the great religions are united in the fundamental principles that they espouse, the Bahá'í writings advocate the moral obligation of everyone to search for truth independently. Religions and beliefs must never be forced on people. Instead, the Bahá'í writings indicate that each individual should utilize his own powers of intellect, reason and spirit to search for truth.

The principle of independent search after truth can help to heal the wounds inflicted by intolerance in at least two important ways. On the one hand, it induces each individual to act humbly towards others, instead of with an air of superiority, and to respect toheir right to choose beliefs of their own as a result of their own quest for truth.

On the other hand, we believe that, if people are permitted to question the dogmas handed down over generations, and to seek truth using their own faculties of perception, they will develop a genuine appreciation for religious tolerance. (Bahá'í International Community, 1988 Feb 17, *Eliminating Religious Intolerance*)

PART II:
THE PATHS

CHAPTER 4:

PATHS FROM JUDAISM TO THE BAHÁ'Í FAITH

FROM THE WRITINGS OF BAHÁ'U'LLÁH

4.1 Consider Moses! Armed with the rod of celestial dominion, adorned with the white hand of Divine knowledge, and proceeding from the Paran of the love of God, and wielding the serpent of power and everlasting majesty, He shone forth from the Sinai of light upon the world. He summoned all the peoples and kindreds of the earth to the kingdom of eternity, and invited them to partake of the fruit of the tree of faithfulness. Surely you are aware of the fierce opposition of Pharaoh and his people, and of the stones of idle fancy which the hands of infidels cast upon that blessed Tree. So much so that Pharaoh and his people finally arose and exerted their utmost endeavor to extinguish with the waters of falsehood and denial the fire of that sacred Tree, oblivious of the truth that no earthly water can quench the flames of Divine wisdom, nor mortal blasts extinguish the lamp of everlasting dominion. Nay, rather, such water cannot but intensify the burning of the flame, and such blasts cannot but ensure the preservation of the lamp, were ye to observe with the eye of discernment, and walk in the way of God's holy will and pleasure...

4.2 The time foreordained unto the peoples and kindreds of the earth is now come. The promises of God, as recorded in the holy Scriptures, have all been fulfilled. Out of Zion hath gone forth the Law of God, and Jerusalem, and the hills and land thereof, are filled with the glory of His Revelation. Happy is the man that pondereth in his heart that which hath been revealed in the Books of God, the Help in Peril, the Self-Subsisting. Meditate upon this, O ye beloved of God, and let your ears be attentive unto His Word, so that ye may, by His grace and mercy, drink your fill from the crystal waters of constancy, and become as steadfast and immovable as the mountain in His Cause.

In the Book of Isaiah it is written: "Enter into the rock, and hide thee in the dust, for fear of the Lord, and for the glory of His majesty." No man that meditateth upon this verse can fail to recognize the greatness of this Cause, or doubt the exalted character of this Day—the Day of God Himself. This same verse is followed by these words: "And the Lord alone shall be exalted in that Day." This is the Day which the Pen of the Most High hath glorified in all the holy Scriptures. There is no verse in them that doth not declare the glory of His holy Name, and no Book that doth not testify unto the loftiness of this most exalted theme. Were We to make mention of all that hath been revealed in these heavenly Books and holy Scriptures concerning this Revelation, this Tablet would assume impossible dimensions. It is incumbent in this Day, upon every man to place his whole trust in the manifold bounties of God, and arise to disseminate, with the utmost wisdom, the verities of His Cause. Then, and only then, will the whole earth be enveloped with the morning light of His Revelation.

4.3 Behold how the people, as a result of the verdict pronounced by the divines of His age, have cast Abraham, the Friend of God, into fire; how Moses, He Who held converse with the Almighty, was denounced as liar and slanderer.

4.4 That which thou hast heard concerning Abraham, the Friend of the All-Merciful, is the truth, and no doubt is there about it. The Voice of God commanded Him to offer up Ishmael as a sacrifice, so that His steadfastness in the Faith of God and His detachment from all else but Him may be demonstrated unto men. The purpose of God, moreover, was to sacrifice him as a ransom for the sins and iniquities of all the peoples of the earth. This same honor, Jesus, the Son of Mary, besought the one true God, exalted be His name and glory, to confer upon Him. For the same reason was Husayn offered up as a sacrifice by Muhammad, the Apostle of God.

No man can ever claim to have comprehended the nature of the hidden and manifold grace of God; none can fathom His all-embracing mercy. Such hath been the perversity of men and their transgressions, so grievous have been the trials that have afflicted the Prophets of God and their chosen ones, that all mankind deserveth to be tormented and to perish. God's hidden and most loving providence, however, hath, through both visible and invisible agencies, protected and will continue to protect it from the penalty of its wickedness. Ponder this in thine heart, that the truth may be revealed unto thee, and be thou steadfast in His path.

4.5 Bestir yourselves, O people, in anticipation of the days of Divine justice, for the promised hour is now come. Beware lest ye fail to apprehend its import and be accounted among the erring.

FROM THE WRITINGS AND UTTERANCES OF 'ABDU'L-BAHÁ

4.6 At a time when the Orient was rent by religious dissension Bahá'u'lláh appeared. He founded teachings which became the means of uniting the various and divergent peoples. He promulgated principles which removed the cause of their dissension, until today in Persia those who had been constantly at war are united. Christians, Muslims, Zoroastrians, Jews—people of every belief and denomination who have followed the teachings of Bahá'u'lláh—have attained complete fellowship and spiritual agreement. Former differences and dissensions have passed away entirely...

4.7 Among the revelators of the law of God was Moses. When He appeared, all the contemporaneous nations rejected Him. Notwithstanding this, single and alone He promulgated the divine teachings and liberated a nation from the lowest condition of degradation and bondage. The people of Israel were ignorant, lowly, debased in morals—a race of slaves under burdensome oppression. Moses led them out of captivity and brought them to the Holy Land. He educated and disciplined them, established among them the foundations of material and divine civilization. Through the education of Moses these ignorant people attained an advanced degree of power and prestige, culminating in the glory of the reign of Solomon. From the abyss of bereavement and slavery they were uplifted to the highest plane of progress and civilized nationhood. It is evident, therefore, that Moses was an Educator and Teacher. The purpose and mission of the holy, divine Messengers is the training and advancement of humanity, the cultivation of divine fruits in the gardens of human hearts, the reflection of heavenly effulgence in the mirrors of human souls, the quickening of mental capacity and the increase of spiritual susceptibilities.

4.8 Verily, I now declare to you that Moses was the Interlocutor of God and a most noteworthy Prophet, that Moses revealed the fundamental law of God and founded the real ethical basis of the civilization and progress of humanity. What harm is there in this? Have I lost anything by saying this to you and believing it as a Bahá'í? On the contrary, it benefits me; and Bahá'u'lláh, the Founder of the Bahá'í Movement, confirms me, saying, "You have been fair and just in your judgment; you have impartially investigated the truth and arrived at a true conclusion; you have announced your belief in Moses, a Prophet of God, and accepted the Torah, the Book of God." Inasmuch as it is possible for me to sweep away all evidences of prejudice by such a liberal and universal statement of belief, why is it not possible for you to do likewise? Why not put an end to this religious strife and establish a bond of connection between the hearts of men? Why should not the followers of one religion praise the Founder or Teacher of another? The other religionists extol the greatness of Moses and admit that He was the Founder of Judaism. Why do the Hebrews refuse to praise and accept the other great Messengers Who have appeared in the world? What harm could there be in this? What rightful objection? None whatever. You would lose nothing by such action and statement. On the contrary, you would contribute to the welfare of mankind. You would be instrumental in establishing the happiness of the world of humanity. The eternal honor of man depends upon the liberalism of this modern age. Inasmuch as our God is one God and the Creator of all mankind, He provides for and protects all. We acknowledge Him as a God of kindness, justice and mercy. Why then should we, His children and followers, war and fight, bringing sorrow and grief into the hearts of each other? God is loving and merciful. His intention in religion has ever been the bond of unity and affinity between humankind.

4.9 In brief, Moses—upon Whom be peace!—founded the law of God, purified the morals of the people of Israel and gave them an impetus toward nobler and higher attainments. But after the departure of Moses, following the decline of the glory of Solomon's era and during the reign of Jeroboam there came a great change in this nation. The high ethical standards and spiritual perfections ceased to exist. Conditions and morals became corrupt, religion was debased, and the perfect principles of the Mosaic law were obscured in superstition and polytheism. War and strife arose among the tribes, and their unity was destroyed. The followers of Jeroboam declared themselves rightful and valid in kingly succession, and the supporters of Rehoboam made the same claim. Finally, the tribes were torn asunder by hostility and hatred, the glory of Israel was eclipsed, and so complete was the degradation that a golden calf was set up as an object of worship in the city of Tyre. Thereupon God sent Elijah, the prophet, who redeemed the people, renewed the law of God and established an era of new life for Israel. History shows a still later change and transformation when this oneness and solidarity were followed by another dispersion of the tribes. Nebuchadnezzar, King of Babylon, invaded the Holy Land and carried away captive seventy thousand Israelites to Chaldea, where the greatest reverses, trials and suffering afflicted these unfortunate people. Then the prophets of God again reformed and reestablished the law of God, and the people in their humiliation again followed it. This resulted in their liberation, and under the edict of Cyrus, King of Persia, there was a return to the Holy City. Jerusalem and the Temple of Solomon were rebuilt, and the glory of Israel was restored. This lasted but a short time; the morality of the people declined, and conditions reached an extreme degree until the Roman general Titus took Jerusalem and razed it to its foundations. Pillage and conquest completed the desolation; Palestine became a waste and wilderness, and the Jews fled from the Holy Land of their ancestors. The cause of this disintegration and dispersion was the departure of Israel from the foundation of the law of God revealed by Moses—namely, the acquisition of divine virtues, morality, love, the development of arts and sciences and the spirit of the oneness of humanity.

4.10 At the time when the Israelites had been dispersed by the power of the Roman Empire and the national life of the Hebrew people had been effaced by their conquerors—when the law of God had seemingly passed from them and the foundation of the religion of God was apparently destroyed—Jesus Christ appeared. When He arose among the Jews, the first thing He did was to proclaim the validity of the Manifestation of Moses. He declared that the Torah, the Old Testament, was the Book of God and that all the prophets of Israel were valid and true. He extolled the mission of Moses, and through His proclamation the name of Moses was spread throughout the world. Through Christianity the greatness of Moses became known among all nations. It is a fact that before the appearance of Christ, the name of Moses had not been heard in Persia. In India they had no knowledge of Judaism, and it was only through the Christianizing of Europe that the teachings of the Old Testament became spread in that region. Throughout Europe there was not a copy of the Old Testament. But consider this carefully and judge it aright: Through the instrumentality of Christ, through the translation of the New Testament, the little volume of the Gospel, the Old Testament, the Torah, has been translated into six hundred languages and spread everywhere in the world. The names of the Hebrew prophets became household words among the nations, who believed that the children of Israel were, verily, the chosen people of God, a holy nation under the especial blessing and protection of God, and that, therefore, the prophets who had arisen in Israel were the daysprings of revelation and brilliant stars in the heaven of the will of God.

4.11 It is an historical fact that during a period of fifteen hundred years the kings of Israel were unable to promulgate broadcast the religion of Judaism. In fact, during that period the name and history of Moses were confined to the boundaries of Palestine and the Torah was a book well known only in that country. But through Christ, through the blessing of the New Testament of Jesus Christ, the Old Testament, the Torah, was translated into six hundred different tongues and spread throughout the world. It was through Christianity that the Torah reached Persia. Before that time there was no knowledge in that country of such a book, but Christ caused its spread and acceptance. Through Him the name of Moses was elevated and revered. He was instrumental in publishing the name and greatness of the Israelitish prophets, and He proved to the world that the Israelites constituted the people of God. Which of the kings of Israel could have accomplished this? Were it not for Jesus Christ, would the Bible, the Torah have reached this land of America? Would the name of Moses be spread throughout the world? Refer to history. Everyone knows that when Christianity was spread, there was a simultaneous spread of the knowledge of Judaism and the Torah. Throughout the length and breadth of

Persia there was not a single volume of the Old Testament until the religion of Jesus Christ caused it to appear everywhere so that today the Holy Bible is a household book in that country. It is evident, then, that Christ was a friend of Moses, that He loved and believed in Moses; otherwise, He would not have commemorated His name and Prophethood. This is self-evident. Therefore, Christians and Jews should have the greatest love for each other because the Founders of these two great religions have been in perfect agreement in Book and teaching. Their followers should be likewise.

4.12 Furthermore, know ye that God has created in man the power of reason, whereby man is enabled to investigate reality. God has not intended man to imitate blindly his fathers and ancestors. He has endowed him with mind, or the faculty of reasoning, by the exercise of which he is to investigate and discover the truth, and that which he finds real and true he must accept. He must not be an imitator or blind follower of any soul. He must not rely implicitly upon the opinion of any man without investigation; nay, each soul must seek intelligently and independently, arriving at a real conclusion and bound only by that reality."

4.13 From this review of the history of the Jewish people we learn that the foundation of the religion of God laid by Moses was the cause of their eternal honor and national prestige, the animating impulse of their advancement and racial supremacy and the source of that excellence which will always command the respect and reverence of those who understand their peculiar destiny and outcome. The dogmas and blind imitations which gradually obscured the reality of the religion of God proved to be Israel's destructive influences, causing the expulsion of these chosen people from the Holy Land of their Covenant and promise.

What, then, is the mission of the divine Prophets? Their mission is the education and advancement of the world of humanity. They are the real Teachers and Educators, the universal Instructors of mankind…

4.14 All down the ages the prophets of God have been sent into the world to serve the cause of truth—Moses brought the law of truth, and all the prophets of Israel after him sought to spread it.

4.15 It was both spiritual and physical. They journeyed to the Promised Land and geography and history both prove that this was a physical journey.

Moses viewed the Promised Land but died before it was reached, having given over his charge to Joshua.

The crossing of the Red Sea has a spiritual meaning. It was a spiritual journey, through and above the sea of corruption and iniquity of the Pharaoh and his people, or army. By the help of God through Moses, the Israelites were able to cross this sea safely and reach the Promised Land (spiritual state) while Pharaoh and his people were drowned in their own corruption.

The Egyptian History recorded even trifling events. Had such a wonderful thing happened as the partings of the physical sea it would also have been recorded.

4.16 It is furthermore a matter of record in numerous historical works that the Philosophers of Greece such as Pythagoras, acquired the major part of their philosophy, both divine and material, from the disciples of Solomon. And Socrates after having eagerly journeyed to meet with some of Israel's most illustrious scholars and divines, on his return to Greece established the concept of the oneness of God and the continuing life of the human soul after it has put off its elemental dust. Ultimately, the ignorant among the Greeks denounced this man who had fathomed the inmost mysteries of wisdom, and rose up to take his life; and then the populace forced the hand of their ruler, and in council assembled they caused Socrates to drink from the poisoned cup.

4.17 You have asked Me a question with regard to the gathering of the children of Israel in Jerusalem in accordance with the prophecy.

Jerusalem, the Holy of Holies, is a revered Temple, a sublime name, for it is the City of God…. The gathering of Israel at Jerusalem means, therefore, and prophecies, that Israel as a whole is gathering beneath the banner of God and will enter the Kingdom of Ancient of Days. For the celestial Jerusalem, which has as its centre, the Holy of Holies, is a City of the Kingdom, a Divine City. The East and West are but a small corner of that City.

Moreover, materially as well (as spiritually), the Israelites will gather in the Holy Land. This is irrefutable prophecy, for the ignominy which Israel has suffered for will-nigh twenty-five hundred years will now be changed into eternal glory, and in the eyes of all, the Jewish people will become glorified to such an extent as to draw the jealousy of its enemies and the envy of its friends.

FROM THE WRITINGS AND LETTERS WRITTEN BY, OR ON BEHALF OF, SHOGHI EFFENDI

4.18 Regarding your question concerning the Jesse from whom Bahá'u'lláh is descended: The Master says in 'Some Answered Questions' referring to Isaiah, chapter 11, verses 1 to 10, that these verses apply 'Word for word to Bahá'u'lláh'. He then identifies this Jesse as the father of David in the following words: '...for Joseph was of the descendants of Jesse the father of David...', thus identifying the Jesse of Isaiah, chapter 11, with being the father of David. Bahá'u'lláh is thus the descendant of Jesse, the father of David.

The Guardian hopes that this will clarify the matter for you. It is a tremendous and fascinating theme, Bahá'u'lláh's connection with the Faith of Judaism, and one which possesses great interest to Jew and Christian alike.

4.19 ...You should certainly endeavour to establish further contacts with your Jewish fellow-citizens, as their spiritual destiny is assuredly bright. The age-long sufferings and tribulations which the Jews all over the world have so cruelly experienced will be terminated during the Bahá'í era, as they will be gradually led to embrace the Faith which, indeed, constitutes the only means of salvation to their race.

4.20 The words Israel, used throughout the Bible, simply refers to the Jewish people, and not to the Chosen ones of this day.

4.21 ... whereas Jerusalem is the spiritual center of Christendom it is not the administrative center of either the Church of Rome or any other Christian denomination. Likewise although it is regarded by Moslems as the spot where one of its most sacred shrines is situated, the Holy Sites of the Muhammadan Faith, and the centre of its pilgrimages, are to be found in Arabia, not in Palestine. The Jews alone offer somewhat of parallel to the attachment which the Bahá'ís have for this country inasmuch as Jerusalem holds the remains of their Holy Temple and was the seat of both the religious and political institutions associated with their past history. But even their cases differs in one respect from that of the Bahá'ís, for it is in the soil of Palestine that the three Central Figures of our religion are buried, and it is not only the centre of Bahá'í pilgrimages from all over the world but also the permanent seat of our Administrative Order...

4.22 He feels you did the right thing to have yourself under 'Religion' registered as a Bahá'í. Unfortunately, owing to this obnoxious and vicious race prejudice of every sort which afflicts the world today, the term Jew has come more to mean a race than a religion. You certainly, as your father feels, should never wish to disassociate yourself from a group of people who have contributed as much to the world as the Jews have. On the other hand your actual religion today is Bahá'í, and he feels that Jews should, when they become Bahá'ís, always give this as their Faith, but as their racial descent they should give 'Jewish'.

FROM THE WRITINGS AND LETTERS WRITTEN BY, OR ON BEHALF OF, THE UNIVERSAL HOUSE OF JUSTICE

4.23 One of the excuses given by Muslims for hostility to the Faith is the location of our world administrative centre in Israel; in the conflict between some Islamic nations and Israel, the Bahá'ís have been accused of being Zionists. It should be made clear that Bahá'ís, who believe in the oneness of humanity and who do not show enmity to any nation, people or creed, cannot take sides in any political controversy. As promoters of genuine love and proclaimers of the unity of mankind, taking sides in such disputes would be diametrically opposed to their religious beliefs. It can be explained, whenever necessary, that Bahá'u'lláh was sent, in 1868, as a Prisoner to the Holy Land by the Ottoman Emperor. For the remainder of His life He was a Prisoner and Exile, and He subsequently passed away near 'Akká in 1892. The holiest Shrines of the Bahá'í Faith, around which its world administrative centre has been established, are situated in the Holy Land because of events which occurred more than half a century before the establishment of Israel and other countries in this part of the world as independent nations. Holy Shrines of the Muslims, Christians and Jews are also located in the Holy Land. Therefore, it is simple enmity to attack the Bahá'í Faith on the basis of the geographical location of its World Centre.

4.24   The Adamic Cycle inaugurated 6000 years ago by the Manifestation of God called Adam is only one of the many bygone cycles. Bahá'u'lláh, as you say, is the culmination of the Adamic Cycle. He is also the Inaugurator of the Bahá'í Cycle.

Obviously there must have been Prophets and Manifestations in the ages preceding the Adamic Cycle. This is supported by the following statement revealed by Bahá'u'lláh.

"And now regarding thy question, 'How is it that no records are to be found concerning the Prophets that have preceded Adam, the Father of Mankind, or of the kings that lived in the days of those Prophets?' Know thou that the absence of any reference to them is no proof that they did not actually exist. That no records concerning them are now available, should be attributed to their extreme remoteness, as well as to the vast changes which the earth hath undergone since their time."

With regard to your question about the creation story, we are asked to quote the following from an unpublished Tablet of 'Abdu'l-Bahá.

'Know ye that the Torah is that which was revealed in the Tablets to Moses, may peace be upon Him, or that to which He was bidden. But the stories are historical narratives and were written after Moses, may peace be upon Him.'

Concerning the story of Adam and Eve, 'Abdu'l-Bahá, in 'Some Answered Questions', explains that it cannot be taken literally. You are asked to refer to pages 122-126 of this book for the symbolic meaning of the story.

CHAPTER 5:

PATHS FROM CHRISTIANITY TO THE BAHÁ'Í FAITH

FROM THE WRITINGS OF BAHÁ'U'LLÁH

5.1   O concourse of priests! Leave the bells, and come forth, then, from your churches. It behoveth you, in this day, to proclaim aloud the Most Great Name among the nations. Prefer ye to be silent, whilst every stone and every tree shouteth aloud: 'The Lord is come in His great glory!'? Well is it with the man who hasteneth unto Him. Verily, he is numbered among them whose names will be eternally recorded and who will be mentioned by the Concourse on High. Thus hath it been decreed by the Spirit in this wondrous Tablet. He that summoneth men in My name is, verily, of Me, and he will show forth that which is beyond the power of all that are on earth. Follow ye the Way of the Lord and walk not in the footsteps of them that are sunk in heedlessness. Well is it with the slumberer who is stirred by the Breeze of God and ariseth from amongst the dead, directing his steps towards the Way of the Lord. Verily, such a man is regarded, in the sight of God, the True One, as a jewel amongst men and is reckoned with the blissful.

5.2   Know thou that when the Son of Man yielded up His breath to God, the whole creation wept with a great weeping. By sacrificing Himself, however, a fresh capacity was infused into all created things. Its evidences, as witnessed in all the peoples of the earth, are now manifest before thee. The deepest wisdom which the sages have uttered, the profoundest learning which any mind hath unfolded, the arts which the ablest hands have produced, the influence exerted by the most potent of rulers, are but manifestations of the quickening power released by His transcendent, His all-pervasive, and resplendent Spirit.

We testify that when He came into the world, He shed the splendor of His glory upon all created things. Through Him the leper recovered from the leprosy of perversity and ignorance. Through Him, the unchaste and wayward were healed. Through His power, born of Almighty God, the eyes of the blind were opened, and the soul of the sinner sanctified.

5.3   Consider the Dispensation of Jesus Christ. Behold, how all the learned men of that generation, though eagerly anticipating the coming of the Promised One, have nevertheless denied Him. Both Annas, the most learned among the divines of His day, and Caiaphas, the high priest, denounced Him and pronounced the sentence of His death.

5.4 And when the days of Moses were ended, and the light of Jesus, shining forth from the dayspring of the Spirit, encompassed the world, all the people of Israel arose in protest against Him. They clamoured that He Whose advent the Bible had foretold must needs promulgate and fulfill the laws of Moses, whereas this youthful Nazarene, who laid claim to the station of the divine Messiah, had annulled the law of divorce and of the Sabbath day—the most weighty of all the laws of Moses. Moreover, what of the signs of the Manifestation yet to come? These people of Israel are even unto the present day still expecting that Manifestation which the Bible hath foretold!

5.5 To them that are endowed with understanding, it is clear and manifest that, when the fire of the love of Jesus consumed the veils of Jewish limitations, and His authority was made apparent and partially enforced, He, the Revealer of the unseen Beauty, addressing one day His disciples, referred unto His passing, and, kindling in their hearts the fire of bereavement, said unto them: "I go away and come again unto you." And in another place He said: "I go and another will come, Who will tell you all that I have not told you, and will fulfil all that I have said." Both these sayings have but one meaning, were ye to ponder upon the Manifestations of the Unity of God with Divine insight.

5.6 Every discerning observer will recognize that in the Dispensation of the Qur'án both the Book and the Cause of Jesus were confirmed. As to the matter of names, Muḥammad, Himself, declared: "I am Jesus." He recognized the truth of the signs, prophecies, and words of Jesus, and testified that they were all of God. In this sense, neither the person of Jesus nor His writings hath differed from that of Muḥammad and of His holy Book, inasmuch as both have championed the Cause of God, uttered His praise, and revealed His commandments. Thus it is that Jesus, Himself, declared: "I go away and come again unto you." Consider the sun. Were it to say now, "I am the sun of yesterday," it would speak the truth. And should it, bearing the sequence of time in mind, claim to be other than that sun, it still would speak the truth. In like manner, if it be said that all the days are but one and the same, it is correct and true. And if it be said, with respect to their particular names and designations, that they differ, that again is true. For though they are the same, yet one doth recognize in each a separate designation, a specific attribute, a particular character. Conceive accordingly the distinction, variation, and unity characteristic of the various Manifestations of holiness, that thou mayest comprehend the allusions made by the Creator of all names and attributes to the mysteries of distinction and unity, and discover the answer to thy question as to why that everlasting Beauty should have, at sundry times, called Himself by different names and titles.

5.7   Leprosy may be interpreted as any veil that interveneth between man and the recognition of the Lord, his God. Whoso alloweth himself to be shut out from Him is indeed a leper, who shall not be remembered in the Kingdom of God, the Mighty, the All-Praised. We bear witness that through the power of the Word of God every leper was cleansed, every sickness was healed, every human infirmity was banished. He it is Who purified the world. Blessed is the man who, with a face beaming with light, hath turned towards Him.

FROM THE WRITINGS AND UTTERANCES OF 'ABDU'L-BAHÁ

5.8   O ye beloved of God! O ye children of His Kingdom! Verily, verily, the new heaven and the new earth are come. The holy City, new Jerusalem, hath come down from on high in the form of a maid of heaven, veiled, beauteous, and unique, and prepared for reunion with her lovers on earth. The angelic company of the Celestial Concourse hath joined in a call that hath run throughout the universe, all loudly and mightily acclaiming: 'This is the City of God and His abode, wherein shall dwell the pure and holy among His servants. He shall live with them, for they are His people and He is their Lord.'

5.9 Reflect upon the past events of the time of Christ, and the present events shall become clear and manifest.

5.10 The treatment ordered by wise physicians of the past, and by those that follow after, is not one and the same, rather doth it depend on what aileth the patient; and although the remedy may change, the aim is always to bring the patient back to health. In the dispensations gone before, the feeble body of the world could not withstand a rigorous or powerful cure. For this reason did Christ say: 'I have yet many things to say unto you, matters needing to be told, but ye cannot bear to hear them now. Howbeit when that Comforting Spirit, Whom the Father will send, shall come, He will make plain unto you the truth.' [1 cf. John 15:26; 16:12-13]

5.11 Material civilization is like a lamp-glass. Divine civilization is the lamp itself and the glass without the light is dark. Material civilization is like the body. No matter how infinitely graceful, elegant and beautiful it may be, it is dead. Divine civilization is like the spirit, and the body gets its life from the spirit, otherwise it becomes a corpse. It has thus been made evident that the world of mankind is in need of the breaths of the Holy Spirit. Without the spirit the world of mankind is lifeless, and without this light the world of mankind is in utter darkness. For the world of nature is an animal world. Until man is born again from the world of nature, that is to say, becomes detached from the world of nature, he is essentially an animal, and it is the teachings of God which convert this animal into a human soul.

5.12 When Christ appeared, twenty centuries ago, although the Jews were eagerly awaiting His Coming, and prayed every day, with tears, saying: 'O God, hasten the Revelation of the Messiah,' yet when the Sun of Truth dawned, they denied Him and rose against Him with the greatest enmity, and eventually crucified that divine Spirit, the Word of God, and named Him Beelzebub, the evil one, as is recorded in the Gospel. The reason for this was that they said: 'The Revelation of Christ, according to the clear text of the Torah, will be attested by certain signs, and so long as these signs have not appeared, whoso layeth claim to be a Messiah is an impostor. Among these signs is this, that the

Messiah should come from an unknown place, yet we all know this man's house in Nazareth, and can any good thing come out of Nazareth? The second sign is that He shall rule with a rod of iron, that is, He must act with the sword, but this Messiah has not even a wooden staff. Another of the conditions and signs is this: He must sit upon the throne of David and establish David's sovereignty. Now, far from being enthroned, this man has not even a mat to sit on. Another of the conditions is this: the promulgation of all the laws of the Torah; yet this man has abrogated these laws, and has even broken the sabbath day, although it is the clear text of the Torah that whosoever layeth claim to prophethood and revealeth miracles and breaketh the sabbath day, must be put to death. Another of the signs is this, that in His reign justice will be so advanced that righteousness and well-doing will extend from the human even to the animal world—the snake and the mouse will share one hole, and the eagle and the partridge one nest, the lion and the gazelle shall dwell in one pasture, and the wolf and the kid shall drink from one fountain. Yet now, injustice and tyranny have waxed so great in His time that they have crucified Him! Another of the conditions is this, that in the days of the Messiah the Jews will prosper and triumph over all the peoples of the world, but now they are living in the utmost abasement and servitude in the empire of the Romans. Then how can this be the Messiah promised in the Torah?'

In this wise did they object to that Sun of Truth, although that Spirit of God was indeed the One promised in the Torah. But as they did not understand the meaning of these signs, they crucified the Word of God. Now the Bahá'ís hold that the recorded signs did come to pass in the Manifestation of Christ, although not in the sense which the Jews understood, the description in the Torah being allegorical. For instance, among the signs is that of sovereignty. For Bahá'ís say that the sovereignty of Christ was a heavenly, divine, everlasting sovereignty, not a Napoleonic sovereignty that vanisheth in a short time. For well nigh two thousand years this sovereignty of Christ hath been established, and until now it endureth, and to all eternity that Holy Being will be exalted upon an everlasting throne.

In like manner all the other signs have been made manifest, but the Jews did not understand. Although nearly twenty centuries have elapsed since Christ appeared with divine splendour, yet the Jews are still awaiting the coming of the Messiah and regard themselves as true and Christ as false.

5.13 In brief, O ye believers of God! The text of the divine Book is this: If two souls quarrel and contend about a question of the divine questions, differing and disputing, both are wrong. The wisdom of this incontrovertible law of God is this: That between two souls from amongst the believers of God, no contention and dispute may arise; that they may speak with each other with infinite amity and love. Should there appear the least trace of controversy, they must remain silent, and both parties must continue their discussions no longer, but ask the reality of the question from the Interpreter. This is the irrefutable command!

5.14 The treatment ordered by wise physicians of the past, and by those that follow after, is not one and the same, rather doth it depend on what aileth the patient; and although the remedy may change, the aim is always to bring the patient back to health. In the dispensations gone before, the feeble body of the world could not withstand a rigorous or powerful cure. For this reason did Christ say: 'I have yet many things to say unto you, matters needing to be told, but ye cannot bear to hear them now. Howbeit when that Comforting Spirit, Whom the Father will send, shall come, He will make plain unto you the truth.'[1]

[1 cf. John 15:26; 16:12-13]

Therefore, in this age of splendours, teachings once limited to the few are made available to all, that the mercy of the Lord may embrace both east and west, that the oneness of the world of humanity may appear in its full beauty, and that the dazzling rays of reality may flood the realm of the mind with light.

The descent of the New Jerusalem denoteth a heavenly Law, that Law which is the guarantor of human happiness and the effulgence of the world of God.

5.15 O thou who hast drawn nigh unto the spirit of Christ in the Kingdom of God! Verily the body is composed of physical elements, and every composite must needs be decomposed. The spirit, however, is a single essence, fine and delicate, incorporeal, everlasting, and of God. For this reason whoso looketh for Christ in His physical body hath looked in vain, and will be shut away from Him as by a veil. But whoso yearneth to find Him in the spirit will grow from day to day in joy and desire and burning love, in closeness to Him, and in beholding Him clear and plain. In this new and wondrous day, it behoveth thee to seek after the spirit of Christ.

Verily the heaven into which the Messiah rose up was not this unending sky, rather was His heaven the Kingdom of His beneficent Lord. Even as He Himself hath said, 'I came down from heaven,'[1] and again, 'The Son of Man is in heaven.'[2] Hence it is clear that His heaven is beyond all directional points; it encircleth all existence, and is raised up for those who worship God. Beg and implore thy Lord to lift thee up into that heaven, and give thee to eat of its food, in this age of majesty and might.

[1 John 6:38]
[2 John 3:13]

5.16 O thou lady of the Kingdom! Praise thou God that in this age, the age of the dispensation of Bahá'u'lláh, thou hast been awakened, hast been made aware of the Manifestation of the Lord of Hosts. All the people of the world are buried in the graves of nature, or are slumbering, heedless and unaware. Just as Christ saith: 'I may come when you are not aware. The coming of the Son of Man is like the coming of a thief into a house, the owner of which is utterly unaware.'

In brief, my hope is that from the bounties of Bahá'u'lláh, thou mayest daily advance in the Kingdom, that thou mayest become a heavenly angel, confirmed by the breaths of the Holy Spirit, and mayest erect a structure that shall eternally remain firm and unshakeable....

These days are very precious; grasp the present opportunity and ignite a candle that shall never be extinguished, and which shall pour out its light eternally illuminating the world of mankind!

5.17 I do not wish to mention the miracles of Bahá'u'lláh, for it may perhaps be said that these are traditions, liable both to truth and to error, like the accounts of the miracles of Christ in the

Gospel, which come to us from the apostles, and not from anyone else, and are denied by the Jews. Though if I wish to mention the supernatural acts of Bahá'u'lláh, they are numerous; they are acknowledged in the Orient, and even by some non-Bahá'ís. But these narratives are not decisive proofs and evidences to all; the hearer might perhaps say that this account may not be in accordance with what occurred, for it is known that other sects recount miracles performed by their founders. For instance, the followers of Brahmanism relate miracles. From what evidence may we know that those are false and that these are true? If these are fables, the others also are fables; if these are generally accepted, so also the others are generally accepted. Consequently, these accounts are not satisfactory proofs. Yes, miracles are proofs for the eyewitness only, and even he may regard them not as a miracle but as an enchantment. Extraordinary feats have also been related of some conjurors.

5.18   From these verses it is obvious that the being of a disciple also is not created by physical power, but by the spiritual reality. The honor and greatness of Christ is not due to the fact that He did not have a human father, but to His perfections, bounties and divine glory. If the greatness of Christ is His being fatherless, then Adam is greater than Christ, for He had neither father nor mother. It is said in the Old Testament, "And the Lord God formed man of the dust of the ground, and breathed into his nostrils the breath of life; and man became a living soul."[1] Observe that it is said that Adam came into existence from the Spirit of life. Moreover, the expression which John uses in regard to the disciples proves that they also are from the Heavenly Father. Hence it is evident that the holy reality, meaning the real existence of every great man, comes from God and owes its being to the breath of the Holy Spirit.

[1 Gen. 2:7.]

The purport is that, if to be without a father is the greatest human glory, then Adam is greater than all, for He had neither father nor mother. Is it better for a man to be created from a living substance or from earth? Certainly it is better if he be created from a living substance. But Christ was born and came into existence from the Holy Spirit.

5.19 The change in conditions, alterations and transformations are necessities of the essence of beings, and essential necessities cannot be separated from the reality of things. So it is absolutely impossible to separate heat from fire, humidity from water, or light from the sun, for they are essential necessities. As the change and alteration of conditions are necessities for beings, so laws also are changed and altered in accordance with the changes and alterations of the times. For example, in the time of Moses, His Law was conformed and adapted to the conditions of the time; but in the days of Christ these conditions had changed and altered to such an extent that the Mosaic Law was no longer suited and adapted to the needs of mankind; and it was, therefore, abrogated. Thus it was that Christ broke the Sabbath and forbade divorce. After Christ four disciples, among whom were Peter and Paul, permitted the use of animal food forbidden by the Bible, except the eating of those animals which had been strangled, or which were sacrificed to idols, and of blood.[1] They also forbade fornication. They maintained these four commandments. Afterward, Paul permitted even the eating of strangled animals, those sacrificed to idols, and blood, and only maintained the prohibition of fornication. So in chapter 14, verse 14 of his Epistle to the Romans, Paul writes: "I know, and am persuaded by the Lord Jesus, that there is nothing unclean of itself: but to him that esteemeth any thing to be unclean, to him it is unclean."

[1 Acts 15:20.]

Also in the Epistle of Paul to Titus, chapter 1, verse 15: "Unto the pure all things are pure: but unto them that are defiled and unbelieving is nothing pure; but even their mind and conscience is defiled."

Now this change, these alterations and this abrogation are due to the impossibility of comparing the time of Christ with that of Moses. The conditions and requirements in the later period were entirely changed and altered. The former laws were, therefore, abrogated.

5.20 Jesus Christ knew this would come to pass and was content to suffer. His abasement was His glorification; His crown of thorns, a heavenly diadem. When they pressed it upon His blessed head and spat in His beautiful face, they laid the foundation of His everlasting Kingdom. He still reigns, while they and their names have become lost and unknown. He is eternal and glorious; they are nonexistent. They sought to destroy Him, but they destroyed themselves and increased the intensity of His flame by the winds of their opposition.

Through His death and teachings we have entered into His Kingdom. His essential teaching was the unity of mankind and the attainment of supreme human virtues through love. He came to establish the Kingdom of peace and everlasting life. Can you find in His words any justification for discord and enmity? The purpose of His life and the glory of His death were to set mankind free from the sins of strife, war and bloodshed.

5.21 Through failure to investigate reality the Jews rejected Jesus Christ. They were expecting His coming; by day and night they mourned and lamented, saying, "O God! Hasten Thou the day of the advent of Christ," expressing most intense longing for the Messiah; but when Christ appeared, they denied and rejected Him, treated Him with arrogant contempt, sentenced Him to death and finally crucified Him. Why did this happen? Because they were blindly following imitations, believing that which had descended to them as a heritage from their fathers and ancestors, tenaciously holding to it and refusing to investigate the reality of Christ.

5.22 A friend asked how the teachings of Bahá'u'lláh contrasted with the teachings of Jesus Christ. "The teachings are the same." declared 'Abdu'l-Bahá; "It is the same foundation and the same temple. Truth is one, and without division. The teachings of Jesus are in a concentrated form. Men do not agree to this day as to the meaning of many of His sayings. His teachings are as a flower in the bud. Today, the bud is unfolding into a flower! Bahá'u'lláh has expanded and fulfilled the teachings, and has applied them in detail to the whole world.

5.23 Without the presence of the Holy Spirit he is lifeless. Although physically and mentally alive, he is spiritually dead. Christ announced, "That which is born of the flesh is flesh; and that which is born of the Spirit is spirit," meaning that man must be born again. As the babe is born into the light of this physical world, so must the physical and intellectual man be born into the light of the world of Divinity.

FROM THE WRITINGS AND LETTERS WRITTEN BY, OR ON BEHALF OF, SHOGHI EFFENDI

5.24 When a person becomes a Bahá'í, he gives up the past only in the sense that he is a part of this new and living Faith of God, and must seek to pattern himself, in act and thought, along the lines laid down by Bahá'u'lláh. The fact that he is by origin a Jew or a Christian, a black man or a white man, is not important anymore, but, as you say, lends color and charm to the Bahá'í community in that it demonstrates unity in diversity.

5.25 A Catholic background is an excellent introduction to the Faith, and one that Mrs. ... should feel gratified for having had. Though doctrines of the church today are no longer needed—as the Father Himself has come, and thus fulfilled the mission of Christ the Son yet the foundation they lay of spiritual discipline, and their emphasis on spiritual values and adherence to moral laws, is very important and very close to our own beliefs.

5.26 Concerning the resurrection of Christ, he wishes to call your attention to the fact that in this as well as in practically all the so-called miraculous events recorded in the Gospel we should, as Bahá'ís, seek to find a spiritual meaning and to entirely discard the physical interpretation attached to them by many of the Christian sects. The resurrection of Christ was, indeed, not physical but essentially spiritual, and is symbolic of the truth that the reality of man is to be found not in his physical constitution, but in his soul. A careful perusal of the Íqán' and of the 'Some Answered Questions' makes this indubitably clear.

FROM THE WRITINGS AND LETTERS WRITTEN BY, OR ON BEHALF OF, THE UNIVERSAL HOUSE OF JUSTICE

5.27 Bahá'ís should obviously be encouraged to preserve their inherited cultural identities, as long as the activities involved do not contravene the principles of the Faith. The perpetuation of such cultural characteristics is an expression of unity in diversity. Although most of these festive celebrations have no doubt stemmed from religious rituals in bygone ages, the believers should not be deterred from participating in those in which, over the course of time, the religious meaning has given way to purely culturally oriented practices. For example, Naw-Rúz itself was originally a Zoroastrian religious festival, but gradually its Zoroastrian connotation has almost been forgotten. Iranians, even after their conversion to Islam, have been observing it as a national festival. Now Naw-Rúz has become a Bahá'í Holy Day and is being observed throughout the world, but, in addition to the Bahá'í observance, many Iranian Bahá'ís continue to carry out their past cultural traditions in connection with this Feast. Similarly, there are a number of national customs in every part of the world which have cultural rather than religious connotations.

In deciding whether or not to participate in such traditional activities, the Bahá'ís must guard against two extremes. The one is to disassociate themselves needlessly from harmless cultural observances and thus alienate themselves from their non-Bahá'í families and friends; the other is to continue the practice of abrogated observances of previous dispensations and thus undermine the independence of the Bahá'í Faith and create undesirable distinctions between themselves and their fellow-Bahá'ís. In this connection there is a difference between what Bahá'ís do among themselves and what they do in companionship with their non-Bahá'í friends and relations.

CHAPTER 6:

PATHS FROM ISLAM TO THE BAHÁ'Í FAITH

FROM THE WRITINGS OF BAHÁ'U'LLÁH

6.1. It is clear and evident to thee that all the Prophets are the Temples of the Cause of God, Who have appeared clothed in divers attire. If thou wilt observe with discriminating eyes, thou wilt behold them all abiding in the same tabernacle, soaring in the same heaven, seated upon the same throne, uttering the same speech, and proclaiming the same Faith. Such is the unity of those Essences of being, those Luminaries of infinite and immeasurable splendour. Wherefore, should one of these Manifestations of Holiness proclaim saying: "I am the return of all the Prophets," He verily speaketh the truth. In like manner, in every subsequent Revelation, the return of the former Revelation is a fact, the truth of which is firmly established. Inasmuch as the return of the Prophets of God, as attested by verses and traditions, hath been conclusively demonstrated, the return of their chosen ones also is therefore definitely proven. This return is too manifest in itself to require any evidence or proof. For instance, consider that among the Prophets was Noah. When He was invested with the robe of Prophethood, and was moved by the Spirit of God to arise and proclaim His Cause, whoever believed in Him and acknowledged His Faith, was endowed with the grace of a new life. Of him it could be truly said that he was reborn and revived, inasmuch as previous to his belief in God and his acceptance of His Manifestation, he had set his affections on the things of the world, such as attachment to earthly goods, to wife, children, food, drink, and the like, so much so that in the day-time and in the night season his one concern had been to amass riches and procure for himself the means of enjoyment and pleasure. Aside from these things, before his partaking of the reviving waters of faith, he had been so wedded to the traditions of his forefathers, and so passionately devoted to the observance of their customs and laws, that he would have preferred to suffer death rather than violate one letter of those superstitious forms and manners current amongst his people. Even as the people have cried: "Verily we found our fathers with a faith, and verily, in their footsteps we follow."[1]

[1 Qur'án 43:22.]

6.2. Every discerning observer will recognize that in the Dispensation of the Qur'án both the Book and the Cause of Jesus were confirmed. As to the matter of names, Muhammad, Himself, declared: "I am Jesus." He recognized the truth of the signs, prophecies, and words of Jesus, and testified that they were all of God. In this sense, neither the person of Jesus nor His writings hath differed from that of Muhammad and of His holy Book, inasmuch as both have championed the Cause of God, uttered His praise, and revealed His commandments. Thus it is that Jesus, Himself, declared: "I go away and come again unto you." Consider the sun. Were it to say now, "I am the sun of yesterday," it would speak the truth. And should it, bearing the sequence of time in mind, claim to be other than that sun, it still would speak the truth. In like manner, if it be said that all the days are but one and the same, it is correct and true. And if it be said, with respect to their particular names and designations, that they differ, that again is true. For though they are the same, yet one doth recognize in each a separate designation, a specific attribute, a particular character. Conceive accordingly the distinction, variation, and unity characteristic of the various Manifestations of holiness, that thou mayest comprehend the allusions made by the creator of all names and attributes to the mysteries of distinction and unity, and discover the answer to thy question as to why that everlasting Beauty should have, at sundry times, called Himself by different names and titles.

6.3. Notwithstanding the obviousness of this theme, in the eyes of those that have quaffed the wine of knowledge and certitude, yet how many are those who, through failure to understand its meaning, have allowed the term "Seal of the Prophets" to obscure their understanding, and deprive them of the grace of all His manifold bounties! Hath not Muhammad, Himself, declared: "I am all the Prophets?" Hath He not said as We have already mentioned: "I am Adam, Noah, Moses, and Jesus?" Why should Muhammad, that immortal Beauty, Who hath said: "I am the first Adam" be incapable of saying also: "I am the last Adam"? For even as He regarded Himself to be the "First of the Prophets"—that is Adam—in like manner, the "Seal of the Prophets" is also applicable unto that

Divine Beauty. It is admittedly obvious that being the "First of the Prophets," He likewise is their "Seal."

The mystery of this theme hath, in this Dispensation, been a sore test unto all mankind. Behold, how many are those who, clinging unto these words, have disbelieved Him Who is their true Revealer. What, We ask, could this people presume the terms "first" and "last"—when referring to God—glorified be His Name!—to mean? If they maintain that these terms bear reference to this material universe, how could it be possible, when the visible order of things is still manifestly existing? Nay, in this instance, by "first" is meant no other than the "last" and by "last" no other than the "first."

Even as in the "Beginning that hath no beginnings" the term "last" is truly applicable unto Him who is the Educator of the visible and of the invisible, in like manner, are the terms "first" and "last" applicable unto His Manifestations. They are at the same time the Exponents of both the "first" and the "last." Whilst established upon the seat of the "first," they occupy the throne of the "last." Were a discerning eye to be found, it will readily perceive that the exponents of the "first" and the "last," of the "manifest" and the "hidden," of the "beginning" and the "seal" are none other than these holy Beings, these Essences of Detachment, these divine Souls. And wert thou to soar in the holy realm of "God was alone, there was none else besides Him," thou wilt find in that Court all these names utterly non-existent and completely forgotten. Then will thine eyes no longer be obscured by these veils, these terms, and allusions. How ethereal and lofty is this station, unto which even Gabriel, unshepherded, can never attain, and the Bird of Heaven, unassisted, can never reach!

6.4. When the Unseen, the Eternal, the divine Essence, caused the Day-star of Muhammad to rise above the horizon of knowledge, among the cavils which the Jewish divines raised against Him was that after Moses no Prophet should be sent of God. Yea, mention hath been made in the scriptures of a Soul Who must needs be made manifest and Who will advance the Faith, and promote the interests of the people, of Moses, so that the Law of the Mosaic Dispensation may encompass the whole earth. Thus hath the King of eternal glory referred in His Book to the words uttered by those wanderers in the vale of remoteness and error: "'The hand of God,' say the Jews, 'is chained up.' Chained up be their own hands! And for that which they have said, they were accursed. Nay, outstretched are both His hands!"[1] "The hand of God is above their hands."[2]

[1 Qur'án 5:64.]
[2 Qur'án 48:10.]

6.5. In like manner, when Muhammad, the Prophet of God—may all men be a sacrifice unto Him—appeared, the learned men of Mecca and Medina arose, in the early days of His Revelation, against Him and rejected His Message, while they who were destitute of all learning recognized and embraced His Faith. Ponder a while. Consider how Balal, the Ethiopian, unlettered though he was, ascended into the heaven of faith and certitude, whilst Abdu'lláh Ubayy, a leader among the learned, maliciously strove to oppose Him. Behold, how a mere shepherd was so carried away by the ecstasy of the words of God that he was able to gain admittance into the habitation of his Best-Beloved, and was united to Him Who is the Lord of Mankind, whilst they who prided themselves on their knowledge and wisdom strayed far from His path and remained deprived of His grace. For this reason He hath written: "He that is exalted among you shall be abased, and he that is abased shall be exalted." References to this theme are to be found in most of the heavenly Books, as well as in the sayings of the Prophets and Messengers of God.

6.6. Leaders of religion, in every age, have hindered their people from attaining the shores of eternal salvation, inasmuch as they held the reins of authority in their mighty grasp. Some for the lust of leadership, others through want of knowledge and understanding, have been the cause of the deprivation of the people. By their sanction and authority, every Prophet of God hath drunk from the chalice of sacrifice, and winged His flight unto the heights of glory.

6.7. How strange! These people with one hand cling to those verses of the Qur'án and those traditions of the people of certitude which they have found to accord with their inclinations and interests, and with the other reject those which are contrary to their selfish desires. "Believe ye then part of the Book, and deny part?"[1] How could ye judge that which ye understand not? Even as the Lord of being hath in His unerring Book, after speaking of the "Seal" in His exalted utterance: "Muhammad is the Apostle of God and the Seal of the Prophets,"[2] hath revealed unto all people the promise of "attainment unto the divine Presence." To this attainment to the presence of the immortal King testify the verses of the Book, some of which We have already mentioned. The one true God is My witness! Nothing more exalted or more explicit than "attainment unto the divine Presence" hath been revealed in the Qur'án. Well is it with him that hath attained thereunto, in the day wherein most of the people, even as ye witness, have turned away therefrom.

[1 Qur'án 2:85.]
[2 Qur'án 33:40.]

6.8. And yet, through the mystery of the former verse, they have turned away from the grace promised by the latter, despite the fact that "attainment unto the divine Presence" in the "Day of Resurrection" is explicitly stated in the Book. It hath been demonstrated and definitely established, through clear evidences, that by "Resurrection" is meant the rise of the Manifestation of God to proclaim His Cause, and by "attainment unto the divine Presence" is meant attainment unto the presence of His Beauty in the person of His Manifestation. For verily, "No vision taketh in Him, but He taketh in all vision."[1] Notwithstanding all these indubitable facts and lucid statements, they have foolishly clung to the term "seal," and remained utterly deprived of the recognition of Him Who is the Revealer of both the Seal and the Beginning, in the day of His presence. "If God should chastise men for their perverse doings, He would not leave upon the earth a moving thing! But to an appointed time doth He respite them."[2] But apart from all these things, had this people attained unto a drop of the crystal streams flowing from the words: "God doeth whatsoever He willeth, and ordaineth whatsoever He pleaseth," they would not have raised any unseemly cavils, such as these, against the focal Center of His Revelation. The Cause of God, all deeds and words, are held within the grasp of His power. "All things lie imprisoned within the hollow of His mighty Hand; all things are easy and possible unto Him." He accomplisheth whatsoever He willeth, and doeth all that He desireth. "Whoso sayeth 'why' or 'wherefore' hath spoken blasphemy!" Were these people to shake off the slumber of negligence and realize that which their hands have wrought, they would surely perish, and would of their own accord cast themselves into fire—their end and real abode. Have they not heard that which He hath revealed: "He shall not be asked of His doings?"[3] In the light of these utterances, how can man be so bold as to question Him, and busy himself with idle sayings?

[1 Qur'án 6:103.]
[2 Qur'án 16:61.]
[3 Qur'án 21:23.]

6.9. These are the melodies, sung by Jesus, Son of Mary, in accents of majestic power in the Ridvan of the Gospel, revealing those signs that must needs herald the advent of the Manifestation after Him. In the first Gospel according to Matthew it is recorded: And when they asked Jesus concerning the signs of His coming, He said unto them: "Immediately after the oppression[1] of those days shall the sun be darkened, and the moon shall not give her light, and the stars shall fall from heaven, and the powers of the earth shall be shaken: and then [1] The Greek word used (Thlipsis) has two meanings: pressure [1] and oppression. shall appear the sign of the Son of man in heaven: and then shall all the tribes of the earth mourn, and they shall see the Son of man coming in the clouds of heaven with power and great glory. And he shall send his angels with a great sound of a trumpet."[1] Rendered into the Persian tongue,[2] the purport of these words is as follows: When the oppression and afflictions that are to befall mankind will have come to pass, then shall the sun be withheld from shining, the moon from giving light, the stars of heaven shall fall upon the earth, and the pillars of the earth shall quake. At that time, the signs of the Son of man shall appear in heaven, that is, the promised Beauty and Substance of life shall, when these signs have appeared, step forth out of the realm of the invisible into the visible world. And He saith: at that time, all the peoples and kindreds that dwell on earth shall bewail and lament, and they shall see that divine Beauty coming from heaven, riding upon the clouds with power, grandeur, and magnificence, sending His angels with a great sound of a trumpet. Similarly, in the three other Gospels, according to Luke, Mark, and John, the same statements are recorded. As We have referred at length to these in Our Tablets revealed in the Arabic tongue, We have made no mention of them in these pages, and have confined Ourselves to but one reference.

[1 Matthew 24:29-31.]

[2 The passage is quoted by Bahá'u'lláh in Arabic and interpreted in Persian.]

Inasmuch as the Christian divines have failed to apprehend the meaning of these words, and did not recognize their object and purpose, and have clung to the literal interpretation of the words of Jesus, they therefore became deprived of the streaming grace of the Muhammadan Revelation and its showering bounties. The ignorant among the Christian community, following the example of the leaders of their faith, were likewise prevented from beholding the beauty of the King of glory, inasmuch as those signs which were to accompany the dawn of the sun of the Muhammadan Dispensation did not actually come to pass. Thus, ages have passed and centuries rolled away, and that most pure Spirit hath repaired unto the retreats of its ancient sovereignty. Once more hath the eternal Spirit breathed into the mystic trumpet, and caused the dead to speed out of their sepulchres of heedlessness and error unto the realm of guidance and grace. And yet, that expectant community still crieth out: When shall these things be? When shall the promised One, the object of our expectation, be made manifest, that we may arise for the triumph of His Cause, that we may sacrifice our substance for His sake, that we may offer up our lives in His path? In like manner, have such false imaginings caused other communities to stray from the Kawthar of the infinite mercy of Providence, and to be busied with their own idle thoughts.

6.10. Beside this passage, there is yet another verse in the Gospel wherein He saith: "Heaven and earth shall pass away: but My words shall not pass away."[1] Thus it is that the adherents of Jesus maintained that the law of the Gospel shall never be annulled, and that whensoever the promised Beauty is made manifest and all the signs are revealed, He must needs re-affirm

and establish the law proclaimed in the Gospel, so that there may remain in the world no faith but His faith. This is their fundamental belief. And their conviction is such that were a person to be made manifest with all the promised signs and to promulgate that which is contrary to the letter of the law of the Gospel, they must assuredly renounce him, refuse to submit to his law, declare him an infidel, and laugh him to scorn. This is proved by that which came to pass when the sun of the Muhammadan Revelation was revealed. Had they sought with a humble mind from the Manifestations of God in every Dispensation the true meaning of these words revealed in the sacred books—words the misapprehension of which hath caused men to be deprived of the recognition of the Sadratu'l-Muntaha, the ultimate Purpose—they surely would have been guided to the light of the Sun of Truth, and would have discovered the mysteries of divine knowledge and wisdom.
[1 Luke 21:33.]

FROM THE WRITINGS AND UTTERANCES OF 'ABDU'L-BAHÁ

6.11. At a time when the Arabian tribes and nomadic peoples were widely separated, living in the deserts under lawless conditions, strife and bloodshed continual among them, no tribe free from the menace of attack and destruction by another—at such a critical time Muhammad appeared. He gathered these wild tribes of the desert together, reconciled, united and caused them to agree so that enmity and warfare ceased. The Arabian nation immediately advanced until its dominion extended westward to Spain and Andalusia.

6.12. Muhammad recognized the sublime grandeur of Christ and the greatness of Moses and the prophets. If only the whole world would acknowledge the greatness of Muhammad and all the Heaven-sent Teachers, strife and discord would soon vanish from the face of the earth, and God's Kingdom would come among men.

The people of Islam who glorify Christ are not humiliated by so doing.

Christ was the Prophet of the Christians, Moses of the Jews—why should not the followers of each prophet recognize and honour the other prophets also? If men could only learn the lesson of mutual tolerance, understanding, and brotherly love, the unity of the world would soon be an established fact.

Bahá'u'lláh spent His life teaching this lesson of Love and Unity. Let us then put away from us all prejudice and intolerance, and strive with all our hearts and souls to bring about understanding and unity between

6.13. From another horizon we see Muhammad, the Prophet of Arabia, appearing. You may not know that the first address of Muhammad to His tribe was the statement, "Verily, Moses was a Prophet of God, and the Torah is a Book of God. Verily, O ye people, ye must believe in the Torah, in Moses and the prophets. Ye must accept all the prophets of Israel as valid." In the Qur'án, the Muslim Bible, there are seven statements or repetitions of the Mosaic narrative, and in all the historic accounts Moses is praised. Muhammad announces that Moses was the greatest Prophet of God, that God guided Him in the wilderness of Sinai, that through the light of guidance Moses hearkened to the summons of God, that He was the Interlocutor of God and the bearer of the tablet of the Ten Commandments, that all the contemporary nations of the world arose against Him and that eventually Moses conquered them, for falsehood and error are ever overcome by truth. There are many other instances of Muhammad's confirmation of Moses. I am mentioning but a few. Consider that Muhammad was born among the savage and barbarous tribes of Arabia, lived among them and was outwardly illiterate and uninformed of the Holy Books of God. The Arabian people were in the utmost ignorance and barbarism. They buried their infant daughters alive, considering this to be an evidence of a valorous and lofty nature. They lived in bondage and serfdom under the Persian and Roman governments and were scattered throughout the desert, engaged in continual strife and bloodshed. When the light of Muhammad dawned, the darkness of ignorance was dispelled from the deserts of Arabia. In a short period of time those barbarous peoples attained a superlative degree of civilization which, with Baghdad as its center, extended as far westward as Spain and afterward influenced the greater part of Europe. What proof of Prophethood could be greater than this, unless we close our eyes to justice and remain obstinately opposed to reason?

Today the Christians are believers in Moses, accept Him as a Prophet of God and praise Him most highly. The Muslims are, likewise, believers in Moses, accept the validity of His Prophethood, at the same time believing in Christ. Could it be said that the acceptance of Moses by the Christians and Muslims has been harmful and detrimental to those people? On the contrary, it has been beneficial to them, proving that they have been fair-minded and just. What harm could result to the Jewish people, then, if they in return should accept Christ and acknowledge the validity of the Prophethood of Muhammad? By this acceptance and praiseworthy attitude the enmity and hatred which have afflicted mankind so many centuries would be dispelled, fanaticism and bloodshed pass away and the world be blessed by unity and agreement. Christians and Muslims believe and admit that Moses was the Interlocutor of God. Why do you not say that Christ was the Word of God? Why do you not speak these few words that will do away with all this difficulty? Then there will be no more hatred and fanaticism, no more warfare and bloodshed in the Land of Promise. Then there will be peace among you forever.

6.14. We entertain no prejudice against Muhammad. Outwardly the Arabian nation was instrumental in overthrowing the Parsi dominion, the sovereignty of Persia. Therefore, the old Parsi nation manifested the utmost contempt toward the Arabs. But we deal justly and will never abandon the standard of fairness. The Arabians were in the utmost state of degradation. They were bloodthirsty and barbarous, so savage and degraded that the Arabian father often buried his own daughter alive. Consider: Could any barbarism be lower than this? The nation consisted of warring, hostile tribal peoples inhabiting the vast Arabian peninsula, and their business consisted in fighting and pillaging each other, making captive women and children, killing each other. Muhammad appeared among such a people. He educated and unified these barbarous tribes, put an end to their shedding of blood. Through His education they reached such a degree of civilization that they subdued and governed continents and nations. What a great civilization was established in Spain by the Muslims! What a marvelous civilization was founded in Morocco by the Moors! What a powerful caliphate or successorship was set up in Baghdad! How much Islam served and furthered the cause of science! Why then should we deny Muhammad? If we deny Him, we awaken enmity and hatred. By our prejudice we become the cause of war and bloodshed, for prejudice was the cause of the tremendous storm which swept through human history for thirteen hundred years and still continues. Even now in the Balkans a commotion is apparent, reflecting it.

The Christian people number nearly three hundred millions and the Muslims about the same. It is no small task to do away with such numbers. And furthermore, why should they be obliterated? For these are all servants of the one God. Let us strive to establish peace between Christians and Muslims. Is it not better? What is the benefit of war? What is its fruitage? For thirteen hundred years there has been warfare and hostility. What good result has been forthcoming? Is it not folly? Is God pleased with it? Is Christ pleased? Is Muhammad? It is evident that They are not. The Prophets have extolled each other to the utmost. Muhammad declared Christ to be the Spirit of God. This is an explicit text of the Qur'án. He declared Christ to be the Word of God. He eulogized the disciples of Christ to the utmost. He bestowed upon Mary, the mother of Christ, the highest praise. Likewise, Christ extolled Moses. He spread broadcast the Old Testament, the Torah, and caused the name of Moses to reach unto the East and the West. The purpose is this: that the Prophets Themselves have manifested the utmost love toward each other, but the nations who believe and follow Them are hostile and antagonistic among themselves.

6.15. A few words concerning the Qur'án and the Muslims: When Muhammad appeared, He spoke of Moses as the great Man of God. In the Qur'án He refers to the sayings of Moses in seven different places, proclaims Him a Prophet and the possessor of a Book, the Founder of the law and the Spirit of God. He said, "Whosoever believes in Him is acceptable in the estimation of God, and whosoever shuns Him or any of the prophets is rejected of God." Even in conclusion He calls upon His own relatives, saying, "Why have ye shunned and not believed in Moses? Why have ye not acknowledged the Torah? Why have ye not believed in the Jewish prophets?" In a certain surih of the Qur'án He mentions the names of twenty-eight of the prophets of Israel, praising each and all of them. To this great extent He has ratified and commended the prophets and religion of Israel. The purport is this: that Muhammad praised and glorified Moses and confirmed Judaism. He declared that whosoever denies Moses is contaminated and even if he repents, his repentance will not be accepted. He pronounced His own relatives infidels and impure because they had denied the prophets. He said, "Because you have not believed in Christ, because you have not believed in Moses, because you have not believed in the Gospels, you are infidels and contaminated." In this way Muhammad has praised the Torah, Moses, Christ and the prophets of the past. He appeared amongst the Arabs, who were a people nomadic and illiterate, barbarous in nature and bloodthirsty. He guided and trained them until they attained a high degree of development. Through His education and discipline they rose from the lowest levels of ignorance to the heights of knowledge, becoming masters of erudition and philosophy. We see, therefore that the proofs applicable to one Prophet are equally applicable to another.

6.16. Christ ratified and proclaimed the foundation of the law of Moses. Muhammad and all the Prophets have revoiced that same foundation of reality. Therefore, the purposes and accomplishments of the divine Messengers have been one and the same. They were the source of advancement to the body politic and the cause of the honor and divine civilization of humanity, the foundation of which is one and the same in every dispensation. It is evident, then, that the proofs of the validity and inspiration of a Prophet of God are the deeds of beneficent accomplishment and greatness emanating from Him. If He proves to be instrumental in the elevation and betterment of mankind, He is undoubtedly a valid and heavenly Messenger.

FROM THE WRITINGS AND LETTERS WRITTEN BY, OR ON BEHALF OF, SHOGHI EFFENDI

6.17. Islam attained a very high spiritual state, but western scholars are prone to judging it by Christian standards. One cannot call one world Faith superior to another, as they all come from God; they are progressive, each suited to certain needs of the times.

6.18. Shoghi Effendi hopes that your lectures will not only serve to deepen the knowledge of the believers in the doctrines and culture and culture of Islam, but will set their hearts afire with the love of everything that vitally pertains to Muhammad and His Faith.

There is so much misunderstanding about Islam in the West in general that you have to dispel. Your task is rather difficult and requires a good deal of erudition. Your chief task is to acquaint the friends with the pure teaching of the Prophet as recorded in the Qur'án, and then to point out how these teachings have, throughout succeeding ages, influenced nay guided the course of human development. In other words you have to show the position and significance of Islam in the history of civilization.

The Bahá'í view on that subject is that the Dispensation of Muhammad, like all other Divine Dispensations, has been fore-ordained, and that as such forms and integral part of the Divine Plan for the spiritual, moral and social, development of mankind, It is not an isolated religious phenomenon, but is closely and historically related to the Dispensation of Christ, and those of the Báb and Bahá'u'lláh. It was intended by God to succeed Christianity, and it was therefore the duty of the Christians to accept it as firmly as they had adhered to the religion of Christ.

You should also cautiously emphasize the truth that due to the historical order of its appearance, and also because of the obviously more advanced character of its teachings, Islam constitutes a fuller revelation of God's purpose for mankind. The so-called Christian civilization of which the Renaissance is one of the most striking manifestations is essentially Muslim in its origins and foundations. When medieval Europe was plunged in darkest barbarism, the Arabs regenerated and transformed by the spirit released by the religion of Muhammad were busily engaged in establishing a civilization the kind of which their contemporary Christians in Europe had never witnessed before. It was eventually through Arabs that civilization was introduced to the West. It was through them that the philosophy, science and culture which the old Greeks had developed found their way to Europe. The Arabs were the ablest translators, and linguists of their age, and it is thanks to them that the writings of such well-known thinkers as Socrates, Plato and Aristotle were made available to the Westerners. It is wholly unfair to attribute the efflorescence of European culture during the Renaissance period to the influence of Christianity. It was mainly the product of the forces released by the Muhammadan Dispensation.

From the standpoint of institutionalism Islam far surpasses true Christianity as we know it in the Gospels. There are infinitely more laws and institutions in the Qur'án than in the Gospel. While the latter's emphasis is mainly, not to say wholly, on individual and personal conduct, the Qur'án stresses the importance of society. This social emphasis acquires added importance and significance in the Bahá'í Revelation. When carefully and impartially compared, the Qur'án marks a definite advancement on the Gospel, from the standpoint of spiritual and humanitarian progress.

The truth is that Western historians have for many centuries distorted the facts to suit their religious and ancestral prejudices. The Bahá'ís should try to study history anew, and to base all their investigations first and foremost on the written Scriptures of Islam and Christianity.

6.19. It is certainly most difficult to thoroughly grasp all the Surihs of the Qur'án, as it requires a detailed knowledge of the social, religious and historical background of Arabia at the time of the appearance of the Prophet. The Believers cannot possibly hope, therefore, to understand the Surihs after the first or even second or third reading. They have to study them again and again, ponder over their meaning, with the help of certain commentaries, and explanatory notes as found, for instance in the admirable translation made by Sale, endeavor to acquire as clear and correct understanding of their meaning and import as possible, This is naturally a slow process, but future generations of believers will certainly come to grasp it. For the present, the Guardian agrees, that it would be easier and more helpful to study the book according to subjects, and not verse by verse and also in the light of Báb, Bahá'u'lláh and 'Abdu'l-Bahá's interpretations which throw such floods of light on the Whole of the Qur'án.

6.20. Regarding your question relative to Surih 4, of the 'Qur'án' in which Muhammad says that the Jews did not crucify Jesus, the Christ but one like Him; what is meant by this passage is that although the Jews succeeded in destroying the physical body of Jesus, yet they were impotent to destroy the Divine reality in Him.

6.21. Concerning the question of plurality of wives among the Muslims; this practice current in all Islamic countries does not conform with the explicit teachings of the Prophet Muhammad. For the Qur'án, while permitting the marriage of more than one wife, positively states that this is conditioned upon absolute Justice. And since absolute justice is impossible to enforce, it follows, therefore, that polygamy can not and should not be practised. The Qur'án, therefore, enjoins monogamy and not polygamy as has hitherto been understood.

6.22. 'Ali's appointment was clear to the Khalifs, who actually disregarded the Prophet's oral statements.
　　　The usurpation occurred immediately after the Prophet's death.
　　　'Ali did not feel unqualified, but wished to avoid schism, which, unfortunately, could not be prevented.
　　　The schisms that have afflicted the religions preceding the Faith of Bahá'u'lláh establish its distinction from all previous Revelations, and single it out among all other Dispensations, as stated by 'Abdu'l-Bahá.
　　　The guidance vouchsafed to the Imams regarding the laws and institutions of Islam was absolute and unqualified. Their infallibility was derived directly from the Manifestation.

The Báb's descent from the Imam Husayn is no doubt a proof of the validity of the Imamate. According to Nabil the dream the Báb had made him first conscious of His Revelation.

The precedence of the name Husayn over 'Ali does establish the greatness of Imam Husayn.

Imam Husayn has, as attested by the Íqán, been endowed with special grace and power among the Imams, hence the mystical reference to Bahá'u'lláh as the return of Imam Husayn, meaning the Revelation in Bahá'u'lláh of those attributes with which Imam Husayn had been specifically endowed.

Joseph was one of the 'Sent Ones, of the Qur'án, meaning a Manifestation of God.

The friends should uphold Islam as a revealed Religion in teaching the Cause but need not make, at present, any particular attempt to teach it solely and directly to non-Bahá'ís at this time.

The mission of the American Bahá'ís is, no doubt to eventually establish the truth of Islam in the West.

The spirit of Islam, no doubt, was the living germ of modern Civilization; which derived its impetus from the Islamic culture in the Middle ages, a culture that was the fruit of the Faith of Muhammad."

FROM THE WRITINGS AND LETTERS WRITTEN BY, OR ON BEHALF OF, THE UNIVERSAL HOUSE OF JUSTICE

6.23. In Iran the officially recognized religious minorities are the adherents of the Jewish, Christian, and Zoroastrian Faiths, although the Bahá'ís outnumber them all. The enemies of the Cause in Iran consider the Bahá'ís as heretical, a 'sect," "cult," or similar group. This is because the Muslims, unlike Bahá'ís who believe in progressive and continuous divine revelation, believe that no prophet will appear after Muhammad. Therefore, whenever Bahá'ís are referred to as a sect or group, the friends should try to remove this misunderstanding and proclaim the independent nature of the Faith to the non-Bahá'í public.

6.24. The Bahá'ís are denounced as "heretics," as "renegades" from Islam, because the Founders of their religion, in the last century, were for the most part, Persian Muslims, because their Prophet, the Báb (1819-1850) had the misfortune to be born after Muhammad, who is considered to be the last Messenger of God. However, the millions of Bahá'ís scattered today in some eighty-eight thousand localities across the five continents are neither of Persian origin nor are they Muslim converts. Beyond this, the Bahá'í Faith recognizes and respects Islam.

6.25. However, the persecutors have "refined" their accusations by "politicizing" them. The Bahá'ís, according to them, are "agents of Israel" because the World Centre of the community is situated in Haifa. But the seat was established in that city in 1868, almost a century before the foundation of the Jewish State.

OTHER SOURCES

6.26. So oft then as an apostle cometh to you with that which your souls desire not, swell ye with pride, and treat some as impostors, and slay others? (Qu'ran, 2:87)

6.27. Those who have bought this worldly life with the Future, the torment shall not be lightened from them nor shall they be helped. We gave Moses the Book and we followed him up with other apostles, and we gave Jesus the son of Mary manifest signs and aided him with the Holy Spirit. Do ye then, every time an apostle comes to you with what your souls love not, proudly scorn him, and charge a part with lying and slay a part? (The Qur'an (E.H. Palmer tr), Sura 2 - The Heifer)

CHAPTER 7:

PATHS FROM HINDUISM TO THE BAHÁ'Í FAITH

FROM THE WRITINGS OF BAHÁ'U'LLÁH

7.1. SON OF DUST! All that is in heaven and earth I have ordained for thee, except the human heart, which I have made the habitation of My beauty and glory; yet thou didst give My home and dwelling to another than Me; and whenever the manifestation of My holiness sought His own abode, a stranger found He there, and, homeless, hastened unto the sanctuary of the Beloved. Notwithstanding I have concealed thy secret and desired not thy shame.

7.2. In every age and cycle He hath, through the splendorous light shed by the Manifestations of His wondrous Essence, recreated all things, so that whatsoever reflecteth in the heavens and on the earth the signs of His glory may not be deprived of the outpourings of His mercy, nor despair of the showers of His favors. How all-encompassing are the wonders of His boundless grace! Behold how they have pervaded the whole of creation. Such is their virtue that not a single atom in the entire universe can be found which doth not declare the evidences of His might, which doth not glorify His holy Name, or is not expressive of the effulgent light of His unity. So perfect and comprehensive is His creation that no mind nor heart, however keen or pure, can ever grasp the nature of the most insignificant of His creatures; much less fathom the mystery of Him Who is the Day Star of Truth, Who is the invisible and unknowable Essence. The conceptions of the devoutest of mystics, the attainments of the most accomplished amongst men, the highest praise which human tongue or pen can render are all the product of man's finite mind and are conditioned by its limitations. Ten thousand Prophets, each a Moses, are thunderstruck upon the Sinai of their search at His forbidding voice, "Thou shalt never behold Me!"; whilst a myriad Messengers, each as great as Jesus, stand dismayed upon their heavenly thrones by the interdiction, "Mine Essence thou shalt never apprehend!" From time immemorial He hath been veiled in the ineffable sanctity of His exalted Self, and will everlastingly continue to be wrapt in the impenetrable mystery of His unknowable Essence. Every attempt to attain to an understanding of His inaccessible Reality hath ended in complete bewilderment, and every effort to approach His exalted Self and envisage His Essence hath resulted in hopelessness and failure.

7.3. And now concerning thy question regarding the soul of man and its survival after death. Know thou of a truth that the soul, after its separation from the body, will continue to progress until it attaineth the presence of God, in a state and condition which neither the revolution of ages and centuries, nor the changes and chances of this world, can alter. It will endure as long as the Kingdom of God, His sovereignty, His dominion and power will endure. It will manifest the signs of God and His attributes, and will reveal His loving kindness and bounty.

7.4. O SON OF BOUNTY! Out of the wastes of nothingness, with the clay of My command I made thee to appear, and have ordained for thy training every atom in existence and the essence of all created things. Thus, ere thou didst issue from thy mother's womb, I destined for thee two founts of gleaming milk, eyes to watch over thee, and hearts to love thee. Out of My loving-kindness, 'neath the shade of My mercy I nurtured thee, and guarded thee by the essence of My grace and favor. And My purpose in all this was that thou mightest attain My everlasting dominion and become worthy of My invisible bestowals. And yet heedless thou didst remain, and when fully grown, thou didst neglect all My bounties and occupied thyself with thine idle imaginings, in such wise that thou didst become wholly forgetful, and, turning away from the portals of the Friend didst abide within the courts of My enemy.

7.5. Certain traditions of bygone ages rest on no foundations whatever, while the notions entertained by past generations, and which they have recorded in their books, have, for the most part, been influenced by the desires of a corrupt inclination.

7.6. It is incumbent upon every man, in this Day, to hold fast unto whatsoever will promote the interests, and exalt the station, of all nations and just governments. Through each and every one of the verses which the Pen of the Most High hath revealed, the doors of love and unity have been unlocked and flung open to the face of men. We have erewhile declared—and Our Word is the truth—: 'Consort with the followers of all religions in a spirit of friendliness and fellowship.' Whatsoever hath led the children of men to shun one another, and hath caused dissensions and divisions amongst them, hath, through the revelation of these words, been nullified and abolished. From the heaven of God's Will, and for the purpose of ennobling the world of being and of elevating the minds and souls of men, hath been sent down that which is the most effective instrument for the education of the whole human race.

7.7. Canst thou discover any one but Me, O Pen, in this Day? What hath become of the creation and the manifestations thereof? What of the names and their kingdom? Whither are gone all created things, whether seen or unseen? What of the hidden secrets of the universe and its revelations? Lo, the entire creation hath passed away! Nothing remaineth except My Face, the Ever-Abiding, the Resplendent, the All-Glorious.

7.8. And now, concerning thy question regarding the creation of man. Know thou that all men have been created in the nature made by God, the Guardian, the Self-Subsisting. Unto each one hath been prescribed a pre-ordained measure, as decreed in God's mighty and guarded Tablets. All that which ye potentially possess can, however, be manifested only as a result of your own volition.

7.9. Praise be unto Thee, O my God! Thou art He Who by a word of His mouth hath revolutionized the entire creation, and by a stroke of His pen hath divided Thy servants one from another. I bear witness, O my God, that through a word spoken by Thee in this Revelation all created things were made to expire, and through yet another word all such as Thou didst wish were, by Thy grace and bounty, endued with new life.

FROM THE WRITINGS AND UTTERANCES OF 'ABDU'L-BAHÁ

7.10. In cycles gone by, each one of the Manifestations of God hath had His own rank in the world of existence, and each hath represented a stage in the development of humanity.

7.11. Love is the most great law that ruleth this mighty and heavenly cycle, the unique power that bindeth together the divers elements of this material world, the supreme magnetic force that directeth the movements of the spheres in the celestial realms. Love revealeth with unfailing and limitless power the mysteries latent in the universe. Love is the spirit of life unto the adorned body of mankind, the establisher of true civilization in this mortal world, and the shedder of imperishable glory upon every high-aiming race and nation.

7.12. Briefly, a return is indeed referred to in the Holy Scriptures, but by this is meant the return of the qualities, conditions, effects, perfections, and inner realities of the lights which recur in every dispensation. The reference is not to specific, individual souls and identities

7.13. What peace, what ease and comfort did the Holy Ones of God ever discover during Their sojourn in this nether world, that They should continually seek to come back and live this life again? Doth not a single turn at this anguish, these afflictions, these calamities, these body blows, these dire straits, suffice, that They should wish for repeated visits to the life of this world? This cup was not so sweet that one would care to drink of it a second time.

7.14. O thou who art voicing the praises of thy Lord! I have read thy letter, wherein thou didst express astonishment at some of the laws of God, such as that concerning the hunting of innocent animals, creatures who are guilty of no wrong.

    Be thou not surprised at this. Reflect upon the inner realities of the universe, the secret wisdoms involved, the enigmas, the inter-relationships, the rules that govern all. For every part of the universe is connected with every other part by ties that are very powerful and admit of no imbalance, nor any slackening whatever. In the physical realm of creation, all things are eaters and eaten: the plant drinketh in the mineral, the animal doth crop swallow down the plant, man doth feed upon the animal, and the mineral devoureth the body of man. Physical bodies are transferred past one barrier after another, from one life to another, and all things are subject to transformation and change, save only the essence of existence itself—since it is constant and immutable, and upon it is founded the life of every species and kind, of every contingent reality throughout the whole of creation.

Whensoever thou dost examine, through a microscope, the water man drinketh, the air he doth breathe, thou wilt see that with every breath of air, man taketh in an abundance of animal life, and with every draught of water, he also swalloweth down a great variety of animals. How could it ever be possible to put a stop to this process? For all creatures are eaters and eaten, and the very fabric of life is reared upon this fact. Were it not so, the ties that interlace all created things within the universe would be unravelled.

And further, whensoever a thing is destroyed, and decayeth, and is cut off from life, it is promoted into a world that is greater than the world it knew before. It leaveth, for example, the life of the mineral and goeth forward into the life of the plant; then it departeth out of the vegetable life and ascendeth into that of the animal, following which it forsaketh the life of the animal and riseth into the realm of human life, and this is out of the grace of thy Lord, the Merciful, the Compassionate.

7.15. Thou hadst asked about fate, predestination and will. Fate and predestination consist in the necessary and indispensable relationships which exist in the realities of things. These relationships have been placed in the realities of existent beings through the power of creation and every incident is a consequence of the necessary relationship. For example, God hath created a relation between the sun and the terrestrial globe that the rays of the sun should shine and the soil should yield. These relationships constitute predestination, and the manifestation thereof in the plane of existence is fate. Will is that active force which controlleth these relationships and these incidents. Such is the epitome of the explanation of fate and predestination. I have no time for a detailed explanation. Ponder over this; the reality of fate, predestination and will shall be made manifest.

7.16. Now observe that in the sensible world appearances are not repeated, for no being in any respect is identical with, nor the same as, another being. The sign of singleness is visible and apparent in all things. If all the granaries of the world were full of grain, you would not find two grains absolutely alike, the same and identical without any distinction. It is certain that there will be differences and distinctions between them. As the proof of uniqueness exists in all things, and the Oneness and Unity of God is apparent in the reality of all things, the repetition of the same appearance is absolutely impossible. Therefore, reincarnation, which is the repeated appearance of the same spirit with its former essence and condition in this same world of appearance, is impossible and unrealizable. As the repetition of the same appearance is impossible and interdicted for each of the material beings, so for spiritual beings also, a return to the same condition, whether in the arc of descent or in the arc of ascent, is interdicted and impossible, for the material corresponds to the spiritual.

7.17. 'Abdu'l-Bahá said: The Message of Krishna is the message of love. All God's prophets have brought the message of love. None has ever thought that war and hate are good. Every one agrees in saying that love and kindness are best.
    Love manifests its reality in deeds, not only in words—these alone are without effect. In order that love may manifest its power there must be an object, an instrument, a motive.

7.18. Blessed souls—whether Moses, Jesus, Zoroaster, Krishna, Buddha, Confucius or Muhammad—were the cause of the illumination of the world of humanity. How can we deny such irrefutable proof? How can we be blind to such light? How can we dispute the validity of Christ? This is injustice. This is a denial of reality. Man must be just. We must set aside bias and prejudice. We must abandon the imitations of ancestors and forefathers. We ourselves must investigate reality and be fair in judgment.

7.19. As humanity progresses, meat will be used less and less, for the teeth of man are not carnivorous. For example, the lion is endowed with carnivorous teeth, which are intended for meat, and if meat be not found, the lion starves. The lion cannot graze; its teeth are of different shape. The digestive system of the lion is such that it cannot receive nourishment save through meat. The eagle has a crooked beak, the lower part shorter than the upper. It cannot pick up grain; it cannot graze; therefore, it is compelled to partake of meat. The domestic animals have herbivorous teeth formed to cut grass, which is their fodder. The human teeth, the molars, are formed to grind grain. The front teeth, the incisors, are for fruits, etc. It is, therefore, quite apparent according to the implements for eating that man's food is intended to be grain and not meat. When mankind is more fully developed, the eating of meat will gradually cease.

7.20. In the eyes of the Creator all His children are equal; His goodness is poured forth on all. He does not favour this nation nor that nation, all alike are His creatures. This being so, why should we make divisions, separating one race from another? Why should we create barriers of superstition and tradition bringing discord and hatred among the people?

The only difference between members of the human family is that of degree. Some are like children who are ignorant, and must be educated until they arrive at maturity. Some are like the sick and must be treated with tenderness and care. None are bad or evil! We must not be repelled by these poor children. We must treat them with great kindness, teaching the ignorant and tenderly nursing the sick.

7.21. Put all your beliefs into harmony with science; there can be no opposition, for truth is one. When religion, shorn of its superstitions, traditions, and unintelligent dogmas, shows its conformity with science, then will there be a great unifying, cleansing force in the world which will sweep before it all wars, disagreements, discords and struggles—and then will mankind be united in the power of the Love of God.

FROM THE WRITINGS AND LETTERS WRITTEN BY, OR ON BEHALF OF, SHOGHI EFFENDI

7.22. He also hopes that the friends in India will do their very best to bring together the Hindus and Mohammedans. In such cases the friends can show their good-will, devotion to humanity, and disinterestedness in the material result obtained.

7.23. As regards your study of the Hindu religion. The origins of this and many other religions that abound in India are not quite known to us, and even the Orientalists and the students of religion are not in complete accord about the results of their investigations in that field. The Bahá'í Writings also do not refer specifically to any of these forms of religion current in India. So, the Guardian feels it impossible to give you any definite and detailed information on that subject. He would urge you, however, to carry on your studies in that field, although its immensity is well-nigh bewildering, with the view of bringing the Message to the Hindus...

7.24. The Hindu and Zoroastrian Bahá'ís should forget their former and traditional prejudices whether religious, racial or social, and commune together on a common basis of equality, love and devotion to the Cause.

7.25. The Bahá'í view of "reincarnation" is essentially different from the Hindu conception. The Bahá'ís believe in the return of the attributes and qualities, but maintain that the essence or the reality of things cannot be made to return. Every being keeps its own individuality, but some of his qualities can be transmitted. The doctrine of metempsychosis upheld by the Hindus is fallacious.

7.26. We know from His Teachings that Reincarnation does not exist. We come on to this planet once only. Our life here is like the baby in the womb of its mother, which develops in that state what is necessary for its entire life after it is born. The same is true of us. Spiritually we must develop here what we will require for the life after death. In that future life, God, through His Mercy, can help us to evolve characteristics which we neglected to develop while we were on this earthly plane. It is not necessary for us to come back and be born into another body in order to advance spiritually and grow closer to God.

This is the Bahá'í Teaching, and this is what the followers of Bahá'u'lláh must accept, regardless of what experiences other people may feel they have. You yourself must surely know that modern psychology has taught that the capacity of the human mind for believing what it imagines, is almost infinite. Because people think they have a certain type of experience, think they remember something of a previous life, does not mean they actually had the experience, or existed previously. The power of their mind would be quite sufficient to make them believe firmly such a thing had happened.

FROM THE WRITINGS AND LETTERS WRITTEN BY, OR ON BEHALF OF, THE UNIVERSAL HOUSE OF JUSTICE

7.27. The Bahá'í community of Bangladesh, flourishing in the midst of a Muslim society, is a source of joy to the entire Bahá'í world. In recent years and with astonishing rapidity, that community began to achieve extraordinary success in the teaching field, and throughout the Three Year Plan it has sustained consistently large-scale expansion. Its institutions have demonstrated their capacity to mobilize the human resources at their disposal, and those who have responded to the call for action have sacrificially and with the utmost devotion spread the Divine Teachings among the Muslim, Hindu and tribal populations of that country. The purity of their motives and the sincerity of their efforts to address the needs of society have won them recognition from government officials in the highest circles. Their exertions to promote love and unity among the majority Muslim and minority Hindu populations are bearing increasing fruit, a striking testimony to the potency of Bahá'u'lláh's Revelation.

7.28. With reference to your question concerning the Sabaean and Hindu religions: there is nothing in the Teachings that could help us in ascertaining which one of these two Faiths is older. Neither history seems to be able to provide a definite answer to this question. The records concerning the origin of these religions are not sufficiently detailed and reliable to offer any conclusive evidence on this point.

7.29. In freeing the believers from the religious rituals of the past and from those customs which are contrary to the Bahá'í principles, the institutions of the Faith should be careful not to press the friends to arbitrarily discard those local tradition which are harmless and often colourful characteristic of particular peoples and tribes....

7.30. Concerning Hindu prophecies of the coming of Bahá'u'lláh and the relationship of the Hindu and Bahá'í Faiths, nothing authentic and specific is available at the World Centre, apart from the Guardian's statement in God Passes By that 'To Him the Bhagavad-Gita of the Hindus had referred as the "Most Great Spirit," the "Tenth Avatar", the "Immaculate Manifestation of Krishna"', (p. 95); and a brief reference to Bahá'u'lláh as 'to the Hindus the reincarnation of Krishna...' (p. 94). Bahá'í teachings on progressive revelation do, of course, bear on the relationship of these Faiths. In a letter written on behalf of the beloved Guardian it is also written that 'We cannot be sure of the authenticity of the scriptures of Buddha and Krishna...' (November 25, 1950); and in reply to a question as to whether Brahma is 'to be considered as referring to absolute deity' and Krishna 'as the Prophet of the Hindu Religion', his secretary wrote '...such matters, as no reference occurs to them in the Teachings, are left for students of history and religion to resolve and clarify.' (April 14, 1941)

OTHER SOURCES

7.31. "When Righteousness
Declines, O Bharata! when Wickedness
Is strong, I rise, from age to age, and take
Visible shape, and move a man with men,
Succouring the good, thrusting the evil back,
And setting Virtue on her seat again."
(*Bhagavad Gita*)

CHAPTER 8:

PATHS FROM BUDDHISM TO THE BAHÁ'Í FAITH

FROM THE WRITINGS OF BAHÁ'U'LLÁH

8.1 O SON OF MAN! Should prosperity befall thee, rejoice not, and should abasement come upon thee, grieve not, for both shall pass away and be no more.

8.2 That which the Lord hath ordained as the sovereign remedy and mightiest instrument for the healing of all the world is the union of all its peoples in one universal Cause, one common Faith.

8.3 O SON OF MY HANDMAID! Be not troubled in poverty nor confident in riches, for poverty is followed by riches, and riches are followed by poverty. Yet to be poor in all save God is a wondrous gift, belittle not the value thereof, for in the end it will make thee rich in God, and thus thou shalt know the meaning of the utterance, "In truth ye are the poor," and the holy words, "God is the all-possessing," shall even as the true morn break forth gloriously resplendent upon the horizon of the lover's heart, and abide secure on the throne of wealth.

8.4 O concourse of monks! If ye choose to follow Me, I will make you heirs of My Kingdom; and if ye transgress against Me, I will, in My long-suffering, endure it patiently, and I, verily, am the Ever-Forgiving, the All-Merciful.

8.5 Say: O concourse of monks! Seclude not yourselves in your churches and cloisters. Come ye out of them by My leave, and busy, then, yourselves with what will profit you and others. Thus commandeth you He Who is the Lord of the Day of Reckoning. Seclude yourselves in the stronghold of My love. This, truly, is the seclusion that befitteth you, could ye but know it. He that secludeth himself in his house is indeed as one dead. It behooveth man to show forth that which will benefit mankind. He that bringeth forth no fruit is fit for the fire. Thus admonisheth you your Lord; He, verily, is the Mighty, the Bountiful. Enter ye into wedlock, that after you another may arise in your stead. We, verily, have forbidden you lechery, and not that which is conducive to fidelity. Have ye clung unto the promptings of your nature, and cast behind your backs the statutes of God? Fear ye God, and be not of the foolish. But for man, who, on My earth, would remember Me, and how could My attributes and My names be revealed?

8.6 To every discerning and illuminated heart it is evident that God, the unknowable Essence, the Divine Being, is immensely exalted beyond every human attribute, such as corporeal existence, ascent and descent, egress and regress. Far be it from His glory that human tongue should adequately recount His praise, or that human heart comprehend His fathomless mystery. He is, and hath ever been, veiled in the ancient eternity of His Essence, and will remain in His Reality everlastingly hidden from the sight of men. "No vision taketh in Him, but He taketh in all vision; He is the Subtile, the All-Perceiving."...

The door of the knowledge of the Ancient of Days being thus closed in the face of all beings, the Source of infinite grace, according to His saying, "His grace hath transcended all things; My grace hath encompassed them all," hath caused those luminous Gems of Holiness to appear out of the realm of the spirit, in the noble form of the human temple, and be made manifest unto all men, that they may impart unto the world the mysteries of the unchangeable Being, and tell of the subtleties of His imperishable Essence.

These sanctified Mirrors, these Day Springs of ancient glory, are, one and all, the Exponents on earth of Him Who is the central Orb of the universe, its Essence and ultimate Purpose. From Him proceed their knowledge and power; from Him is derived their sovereignty. The beauty of their countenance is but a reflection of His image, and their revelation a sign of His deathless glory. They are the Treasuries of Divine knowledge, and the Repositories of celestial wisdom. Through them is transmitted a grace that is infinite, and by them is revealed the Light that can never fade.... These Tabernacles of Holiness, these Primal Mirrors which reflect the light of unfading glory, are but expressions of Him Who is the Invisible of the Invisibles. By the revelation of these Gems of Divine virtue all the names and attributes of God, such as knowledge and power, sovereignty and dominion, mercy and wisdom, glory, bounty, and grace, are made manifest.

These attributes of God are not, and have never been, vouchsafed specially unto certain Prophets, and withheld from others. Nay, all the Prophets of God, His well-favored, His holy and chosen Messengers are, without exception, the bearers of His names, and the embodiments of His attributes. They only differ in the intensity of their revelation, and the comparative potency of their light. Even as He hath revealed: "Some of the Apostles We have caused to excel the others."

8.7 O FRIENDS! Abandon not the everlasting beauty for a beauty that must die, and set not your affections on this mortal world of dust.

8.8 O SON OF MAN! Thou dost wish for gold and I desire thy freedom from it. Thou thinkest thyself rich in its possession, and I recognize thy wealth in thy sanctity therefrom. By My life! This is My knowledge, and that is thy fancy; how can My way accord with thine?

8.9 O MY SERVANT! Free thyself from the fetters of this world, and loose thy soul from the prison of self. Seize thy chance, for it will come to thee no more.

8.10 Glorified, immeasurably glorified art Thou, in Whose hands is the empire of whatsoever is in the heavens and whatsoever is on earth, Thou, Who through but one word of Thy mouth, caused all things to expire and dissolve asunder, and Who, by yet another word, caused whatever had been separated to be combined and reunited!

8.11 By self-surrender and perpetual union with God is meant that men should merge their will wholly in the Will of God, and regard their desires as utter nothingness beside His Purpose. Whatsoever the Creator commandeth His creatures to observe, the same must they diligently, and with the utmost joy and eagerness, arise and fulfil. They should in no wise allow their fancy to obscure their judgment, neither should they regard their own imaginings as the voice of the Eternal. In the Prayer of Fasting We have revealed: "Should Thy Will decree that out of Thy mouth these words proceed and be addressed unto them, 'Observe, for My Beauty's sake, the fast, O people, and set no limit to its duration,' I swear by the majesty of Thy glory, that every one of them will faithfully observe it, will abstain from whatsoever will violate Thy law, and will continue to do so until they yield up their souls unto Thee." In this consisteth the complete surrender of one's will to the Will of God. Meditate on this, that thou mayest drink in the waters of everlasting life which flow through the words of the Lord of all mankind, and mayest testify that the one true God hath ever been immeasurably exalted above His creatures. He, verily, is the Incomparable, the Ever-Abiding, the Omniscient, the All-Wise. The station of absolute self-surrender transcendeth, and will ever remain exalted above, every other station.

It behoveth thee to consecrate thyself to the Will of God. Whatsoever hath been revealed in His Tablets is but a reflection of His Will. So complete must be thy consecration, that every trace of worldly desire will be washed from thine heart. This is the meaning of true unity.

FROM THE WRITINGS AND UTTERANCES OF 'ABDU'L-BAHÁ

8.12   Regarding the statement in The Hidden Words, that man must renounce his own self, the meaning is that he must renounce his inordinate desires, his selfish purposes and the promptings of his human self, and seek out the holy breathings of the spirit, and follow the yearnings of his higher self, and immerse himself in the sea of sacrifice, with his heart fixed upon the beauty of the All-Glorious.

8.13   Thou hast indeed examined with great care the reasons for the incursion of disease into the human body. It is certainly the case that sins are a potent cause of physical ailments. If humankind were free from the defilements of sin and waywardness, and lived according to a natural, inborn equilibrium, without following wherever their passions led, it is undeniable that diseases would no longer take the ascendant, nor diversify with such intensity.

But man hath perversely continued to serve his lustful appetites, and he would not content himself with simple foods. Rather, he prepared for himself food that was compounded of many ingredients, of substances differing one from the other. With this, and with the perpetrating of vile and ignoble acts, his attention was engrossed, and he abandoned the temperance and moderation of a natural way of life. The result was the engendering of diseases both violent and diverse.

8.14 How good it is if the friends be as close as sheaves of light, if they stand together side by side in a firm unbroken line. For now have the rays of reality from the Sun of the world of existence, united in adoration all the worshippers of this light; and these rays have, through infinite grace, gathered all peoples together within this wide-spreading shelter; therefore must all souls become as one soul, and all hearts as one heart. Let all be set free from the multiple identities that were born of passion and desire, and in the oneness of their love for God find a new way of life.

8.15 The founder of Buddhism was a wonderful soul. He established the Oneness of God, but later the original principles of His doctrines gradually disappeared, and ignorant customs and ceremonials arose and increased until they finally ended in the worship of statues and images.

8.16 Unless one accepts dire vicissitudes, he will not attain. To me prison is freedom, troubles rest me, death is life, and to be despised is honour. Therefore, I was happy all that time in prison. When one is released from the prison of self, that is indeed release, for that is the greater prison. When this release takes place, then one cannot be outwardly imprisoned. When they put my feet in stocks, I would say to the guard, 'You cannot imprison me, for here I have light and air and bread and water. There will come a time when my body will be in the ground, and I shall have neither light nor air nor food nor water, but even then I shall not be imprisoned.' The afflictions which come to humanity sometimes tend to centre the consciousness upon the limitations, and this is a veritable prison. Release comes by making of the will a Door through which the confirmations of the Spirit come.

8.17 Such is this mortal abode—a storehouse of afflictions and suffering. It is negligence that binds man to it for no comfort can be secured by any soul in this world, from monarch down to the least subject. If once it should offer man a sweet cup, a hundred bitter ones will follow it and such is the condition of this world. The wise man therefore does not attach himself to this mortal life and does not depend upon it...

8.18 If we suffer it is the outcome of material things, and all the trials and troubles come from this world of illusion.

8.19 Man possesses two kinds of susceptibilities: the natural emotions, which are like dust upon the mirror, and spiritual susceptibilities, which are merciful and heavenly characteristics.
There is a power which purifies the mirror from dust and transforms its reflection into intense brilliancy and radiance so that spiritual susceptibilities may chasten the hearts and heavenly bestowals sanctify them. What is the dust which obscures the mirror? It is attachment to the world, avarice, envy, love of luxury and comfort, haughtiness and self-desire; this is the dust which prevents reflection of the rays of the Sun of Reality in the mirror. The natural emotions are blameworthy and are like rust which deprives the heart of the bounties of God. But sincerity, justice, humility, severance, and love for the believers of God will purify the mirror and make it radiant with reflected rays from the Sun of Truth.

8.20 Therefore, rebirth means his release from the captivity of nature, freedom from attachment to this mortal and material life. This is the second, or spiritual, birth of which Jesus Christ spoke in the Gospels.

8.21 The majority of people are captives in the matrix of nature, submerged in the sea of materiality. We must pray that they may be reborn, that they may attain insight and spiritual hearing, that they may receive the gift of another heart, a new transcendent power, and in the eternal world the unending bestowal of divine bounties.

8.22 O Lord! Make us useful in this world; free us from the condition of self and desire.

8.23 For I have heard that this is an open forum, investigating reality; that you are free from blind imitations, desiring to arrive at the truth of things, and that your endeavors are lofty.

8.24 There are no solitaries and no hermits among the Bahá'ís. Man must work with his fellows. Everyone should have some trade, or art or profession, be he rich or poor, and with this he must serve humanity. This service is acceptable as the highest form of worship.

8.25 The candle of Buddha is shining.

8.26 Some referred to the teaching of Buddha. 'Abdu'l-Bahá said: The real teaching of Buddha is the same as the teaching of Jesus Christ. The teachings of all the Prophets are the same in character. Now men have changed the teaching. If you look at the present practice of the Buddhist religion, you will see that there is little of the Reality left. Many worship idols although their teaching forbids it.

   Buddha had disciples and he wished to send them out into the world to teach, so he asked them questions to see if they were prepared as he would have them be. "When you go to the East and to the West," said the Buddha, "and the people shut their doors to you and refuse to speak to you, what will you do?"—The disciples answered and said: "We shall be very thankful that they do us no harm."—"Then if they do you harm and mock, what will you do?"—"We shall be very thankful that they do not give us worse treatment."—"If they throw you into prison?"—"We shall still be grateful that they do not kill us."—"What if they were to kill you?" the Master asked for the last time. "Still," answered the disciples, "we will be thankful, for they cause us to be martyrs. What more glorious fate is there than this, to die for the glory of God?" And the Buddha said: "Well done!"

   The teaching of Buddha was like a young and beautiful child, and now it has become as an old and decrepit man. Like the aged man it cannot see, it cannot hear, it cannot remember anything. Why go so far back? Consider the laws of the Old Testament: the Jews do not follow Moses as their example nor keep his commands. So it is with many other religions.

FROM THE WRITINGS AND LETTERS WRITTEN BY, OR ON BEHALF OF, SHOGHI EFFENDI

8.27 He alone is meant by the prophecy attributed to Gautama Buddha Himself, that "a Buddha named Maitreye, the Buddha of universal fellowship" should, in the fullness of time, arise and reveal "His boundless glory." To Him the Bhagavad-Gita of the Hindus had referred as the "Most Great Spirit," the "Tenth Avatar," the "Immaculate Manifestation of Krishna."

8.28 The Buddha was a Manifestation of God, like Christ, but His followers do not possess His authentic Writings.

FROM THE WRITINGS AND LETTERS WRITTEN BY, OR ON BEHALF OF, THE UNIVERSAL HOUSE OF JUSTICE

8.29 Among your peoples, the majority of whom have been influenced by noble and high-minded teachings of Buddhism, are many who possess a profound sense of spirituality, which is reflected in the practices of their daily lives and in the quality of their relationships with one another, with nature, and with their social institutions. They have a keen understanding of the need for coherence between the material and the spiritual, and are disturbed by the effects of gross materialism on their societies in recent years. Your region represents a vast reservoir of potential promoters of the Cause waiting to be tapped. The number and quality of the active supporters of the Faith with which it is already blessed bespeak the richness of that reservoir.

8.30 Dear Friends, any attempt to present, no matter how briefly, an overview of the potentialities of your region must necessarily take into account the preponderating influence that the Chinese people are to exert on the destiny of humankind. To them, 'Abdu'l-Bahá has referred as "truth-seeking" and "prompted with ideal motives". From among them, He declared, can be raised "such divine personages that each one of them may become the bright candle of the world of humanity." The progress of the Faith in Hong Kong, Macau and Taiwan, and the labours of the Chinese believers resident in other parts of the region, are early indications of that which is yet to come. We turn our expectant eyes towards the Chinese people, confident in their ability to become illumined with the light of Bahá'u'lláh's Revelation and to apply His Teachings, with characteristic diligence, to the advancement of spiritual and material civilization. As larger and larger numbers become imbued with heavenly qualities, and as they make sincere exertions for the progress of their people, they shall, God willing, win the trust of fair-minded leaders and be able to broaden the scope of their endeavours in a land that 'Abdu'l-Bahá has designated "the country of the future".

OTHER SOURCES

8.31 I am not the first Buddha Who came upon this earth, nor shall I be the last. In due time, another Buddha will arise in the world, a Holy One, a supremely enlightened One... knowing the universe, an Incomparable Leader of men... He will reveal to you the same eternal truths which I have taught you. He will preach to you His religion, glorious in its origin, glorious at the climax and glorious at the goal... He will proclaim a religious life, wholly perfect and pure, such as I now proclaim. His disciples will number many thousands, while mine number many hundreds. (*Digha-nikaya*, IV.26).

8.32 In due time, O monks, there will arise in the world an Exalted One named Mettaya, an arahat, fully awakened, full of wisdom and a perfect guide, himself having trodden the path to the very end, with knowledge of the worlds, unsurpassed as an educator, teacher of gods and men, an exalted Buddha, just as in the present period I am now ... And he will proclaim the teaching that is lovely in its origin, lovely in its progress, and lovely in its consummation ... (DN, *Mahaparinibbana-Suttana* 3:76)

8.33 Then the Blessed One spoke and said: Know, Vasettha, that from time to time a Tathagata [Lord] is born into the world, a fully Enlightened One, blessed and worthy, abounding in wisdom and goodness, happy with knowledge of the worlds, unsurpassed as a guide to erring mortals, a teacher of gods and men, a Blessed Buddha. He thoroughly understands this universe, as though he saw it face to face—the world below with all its people, the worlds above, of Mara and of Brahma—and all creatures, Samanas and Brahmans, gods and men, and from that knowledge makes it known and teaches others. The Truth does he proclaim both in its letter and in its spirit, lovely in its origin, lovely in its progress, lovely in its consummation. A higher life doth he make known in all its purity and in all its perfectness. (*Tevigga Sutra, 'Buddhist Bible'*, Dwight Goddard translations)

8.34 All Buddhas and Tathagatas from their very beginnings have developed hearts of Compassion and have spontaneously manifested Paramitas of charity, unselfish kindness, humility and patience, zeal and perseverance, tranquility and Wisdom, not for any gain to themselves but for the sake of all sentient beings. They have made great Vows, dedicating themselves to emancipating all sentient beings from their bondage to the world of sense. But the deliverance is effected not by outer acts but by an inner drawing of spirit not limited by time or conditions, but is ceaseless even to infinite ages of the future. The activity of Buddhas and Tathagatas is eternal because it is the opposite of outer activities of false mind which are subject to weariness and inertia. Its activities release and store up energy restoring the original purity and unity and peacefulness. (*Awakening of Faith, 'Buddhist Bible'*, Dwight Goddard translations)

CHAPTER 9:

PATHS FROM NATIVE RELIGIONS TO THE BAHÁ'Í FAITH

FROM THE WRITINGS OF BAHÁ'U'LLÁH

9.1 By Thy glory! Every time I lift up mine eyes unto Thy heaven, I call to mind Thy highness and Thy loftiness, and Thine incomparable glory and greatness; and every time I turn my gaze to Thine earth, I am made to recognize the evidences of Thy power and the tokens of Thy bounty. And when I behold the sea, I find that it speaketh to me of Thy majesty, and of the potency of Thy might, and of Thy sovereignty and Thy grandeur. And at whatever time I contemplate the mountains, I am led to discover the ensigns of Thy victory and the standards of Thine omnipotence.

9.2 Every man of discernment, while walking upon the earth, feeleth indeed abashed, inasmuch as he is fully aware that the thing which is the source of his prosperity, his wealth, his might, his exaltation, his advancement and power is, as ordained by God, the very earth which is trodden beneath the feet of all men. There can be no doubt that whoever is cognizant of this truth, is cleansed and sanctified from all pride, arrogance, and vainglory.

9.3 O CHILDREN OF MEN! Know ye not why We created you all from the same dust? That no one should exalt himself over the other. Ponder at all times in your hearts how ye were created. Since We have created you all from one same substance it is incumbent on you to be even as one soul, to walk with the same feet, eat with the same mouth and dwell in the same land, that from your inmost being, by your deeds and actions, the signs of oneness and the essence of detachment may be made manifest. Such is My counsel to you, O concourse of light! Heed ye this counsel that ye may obtain the fruit of holiness from the tree of wondrous glory.

9.4 Look not upon the creatures of God except with the eye of kindliness and of mercy, for Our loving providence hath pervaded all created things, and Our grace encompassed the earth and the heavens.

9.5 Know thou, moreover, that in this most hallowed and resplendent city thou shalt find the wayfarer to be lowly before all men and humble before all things. For naught doth he behold save that he perceiveth God therein. He beholdeth the effulgent glories of God in the lights of His Revelation that have encompassed the Sinai of creation. In this station the wayfarer must not claim the seat of honour in any gathering or walk before others in the desire to vaunt and exalt himself. Rather must he regard himself as standing at all times in the presence of his Lord. He must not wish for anyone that which he doth not wish for himself, nor speak that which he would not bear to hear spoken by another, nor yet desire for any soul that which he would not have desired for himself. It befitteth him, rather, to walk upon the earth with undeviating steps in the kingdom of His new creation.

9.6 They who are the beloved of God, in whatever place they gather and whomsoever they may meet, must evince, in their attitude towards God, and in the manner of their celebration of His praise and glory, such humility and submissiveness that every atom of the dust beneath their feet may attest the depth of their devotion. The conversation carried by these holy souls should be informed with such power that these same atoms of dust will be thrilled by its influence. They should conduct themselves in such manner that the earth upon which they tread may never be allowed to address to them such words as these: "I am to be preferred above you. For witness, how patient I am in bearing the burden which the husbandman layeth upon me. I am the instrument that continually imparteth unto all beings the blessings with which He Who is the Source of all grace hath entrusted me. Notwithstanding the honor conferred upon me, and the unnumbered evidences of my wealth—a wealth that supplieth the needs of all creation—behold the measure of my humility, witness with what absolute submissiveness I allow myself to be trodden beneath the feet of men....

9.7 Know thou that We have annulled the rule of the sword, as an aid to Our Cause, and substituted for it the power born of the utterance of men. Thus have We irrevocably decreed, by virtue of Our grace. Say: O people! Sow not the seeds of discord among men, and refrain from contending with your neighbor, for your Lord hath committed the world and the cities thereof to the care of the kings of the earth, and made them the emblems of His own power, by virtue of the sovereignty He hath chosen to bestow upon them. He hath refused to reserve for Himself any share whatever of this world's dominion. To this He Who is Himself the Eternal Truth will testify. The things He hath reserved for Himself are the cities of men's hearts, that He may cleanse them from all earthly defilements, and enable them to draw nigh unto the hallowed Spot which the hands of the infidel can never profane. Open, O people, the city of the human heart with the key of your utterance. Thus have We, according to a pre-ordained measure, prescribed unto you your duty.

9.8 O SON OF DUST! The wise are they that speak not unless they obtain a hearing, even as the cup-bearer, who proffereth not his cup till he findeth a seeker, and the lover who crieth not out from the depths of his heart until he gazeth upon the beauty of his beloved. Wherefore sow the seeds of wisdom and knowledge in the pure soil of the heart, and keep them hidden, till the hyacinths of divine wisdom spring from the heart and not from mire and clay.

9.9 O MY FRIENDS! Walk ye in the ways of the good pleasure of the Friend, and know that His pleasure is in the pleasure of His creatures. That is: no man should enter the house of his friend save at his friend's pleasure, nor lay hands upon his treasures nor prefer his own will to his friend's, and in no wise seek an advantage over him. Ponder this, ye that have insight!

9.10 O SON OF SPIRIT! The bird seeketh its nest; the nightingale the charm of the rose; whilst those birds, the hearts of men, content with transient dust, have strayed far from their eternal nest, and with eyes turned towards the slough of heedlessness are bereft of the glory of the divine presence. Alas! How strange and pitiful; for a mere cupful, they have turned away from the billowing seas of the Most High, and remained far from the most effulgent horizon.

9.11 The country is the world of the soul, the city is the world of the bodies.

9.12 The fundamental purpose animating the Faith of God and His Religion is to safeguard the interests and promote the unity of the human race, and to foster the spirit of love and fellowship amongst men. Suffer it not to become a source of dissension and discord, of hate and enmity.

FROM THE WRITINGS AND UTTERANCES OF 'ABDU'L-BAHÁ

9.13 You must attach great importance to the Indians, the original inhabitants of America... . Should these Indians be educated and properly guided, there can be no doubt that through the Divine teachings they will become so enlightened that the whole earth will be illumined.

9.14 O ye the sincere loved ones of the Abha Beauty! In these days the Cause of God, the world over, is fast growing in power and, day by day, is spreading further and further to the utmost bounds of the earth. Its enemies, therefore, from all the kindreds and peoples of the world, are growing aggressive, malevolent, envious and bitterly hostile. It is incumbent upon the loved ones of God to exercise the greatest care and prudence in all things, whether great or small, to take counsel together and unitedly resist the onslaught of the stirrers up of strife and the movers of mischief. They must endeavour to consort in a friendly spirit with everyone, must follow moderation in their conduct, must have respect and consideration one for another and show loving-kindness and tender regard to all the peoples of the world. They must be patient and long-suffering, that they may grow to become the divine magnets of the Abha Kingdom and acquire the dynamic power of the hosts of the realm on high.

9.15 Let all your striving be for this, to become the source of life and immortality, and peace and comfort and joy, to every human soul, whether one known to you or a stranger, one opposed to you or on your side. Look ye not upon the purity or impurity of his nature: look ye upon the all-embracing mercy of the Lord, the light of Whose grace hath embosomed the whole earth and all who dwell thereon, and in the plenitude of Whose bounty are immersed both the wise and the ignorant. Stranger and friend alike are seated at the table of His favour. Even as the believer, the denier who turneth away from God doth at the same time cup his hands and drink from the sea of His bestowals.

It behoveth the loved ones of the Lord to be the signs and tokens of His universal mercy and the embodiments of His own excelling grace. Like the sun, let them cast their rays upon garden and rubbish heap alike, and even as clouds in spring, let them shed down their rain upon flower and thorn. Let them seek but love and faithfulness, let them not follow the ways of unkindness, let their talk be confined to the secrets of friendship and of peace. Such are the attributes of the righteous, such is the distinguishing mark of those who serve His Threshold.

9.16 It is incumbent upon you to ponder in your hearts and meditate upon His words, and humbly to call upon Him, and to put away self in His heavenly Cause. These are the things that will make of you signs of guidance unto all mankind, and brilliant stars shining down from the all-highest horizon, and towering trees in the Abha Paradise.

9.17 In cycles gone by, though harmony was established, yet, owing to the absence of means, the unity of all mankind could not have been achieved. Continents remained widely divided, nay even among the peoples of one and the same continent association and interchange of thought were wellnigh impossible. Consequently intercourse, understanding and unity amongst all the peoples and kindreds of the earth were unattainable. In this day, however, means of communication have multiplied, and the five continents of the earth have virtually merged into one. And for everyone it is now easy to travel to any land, to associate and exchange views with its peoples, and to become familiar, through publications, with the conditions, the religious beliefs and the thoughts of all men. In like manner all the members of the human family, whether peoples or governments, cities or villages, have become increasingly interdependent. For none is self-sufficiency any longer possible, inasmuch as political ties unite all peoples and nations, and the bonds of trade and industry, of agriculture and education, are being strengthened every day. Hence the unity of all mankind can in this day be achieved. Verily this is none other but one of the wonders of this wondrous age, this glorious century. Of this past ages have been deprived, for this century—the century of light—hath been endowed with unique and unprecedented glory, power and illumination. Hence the miraculous unfolding of a fresh marvel every day. Eventually it will be seen how bright its candles will burn in the assemblage of man.

9.18 This is a new cycle of human power. All the horizons of the world are luminous, and the world will become indeed as a garden and a paradise. It is the hour of unity of the sons of men and of the drawing together of all races and all classes. You are loosed from ancient superstitions which have kept men ignorant, destroying the foundation of true humanity.

9.19 O Thou kind Lord! Thou hast created all humanity from the same stock. Thou hast decreed that all shall belong to the same household. In Thy Holy Presence they are all Thy servants, and all mankind are sheltered beneath Thy Tabernacle; all have gathered together at Thy Table of Bounty; all are illumined through the light of Thy Providence.

O God! Thou art kind to all, Thou hast provided for all, dost shelter all, conferrest life upon all. Thou hast endowed each and all with talents and faculties, and all are submerged in the Ocean of Thy Mercy.

O Thou kind Lord! Unite all. Let the religions agree and make the nations one, so that they may see each other as one family and the whole earth as one home. May they all live together in perfect harmony.

O God! Raise aloft the banner of the oneness of mankind.

O God! Establish the Most Great Peace.

Cement Thou, O God, the hearts together.

O Thou kind Father, God! Gladden our hearts through the fragrance of Thy love. Brighten our eyes through the Light of Thy Guidance. Delight our ears with the melody of Thy Word, and shelter us all in the Stronghold of Thy Providence.

Thou art the Mighty and Powerful, Thou art the Forgiving and Thou art the One Who overlooketh the shortcomings of all mankind

FROM THE WRITINGS AND LETTERS WRITTEN BY, OR ON BEHALF OF, SHOGHI EFFENDI

9.20 How often—and the early history of the Faith in the land of its birth offers many a striking testimony—have the lowliest adherents of the Faith, unschooled and utterly inexperienced, and with no standing whatever, and in some cases devoid of intelligence, been capable of winning victories for their Cause, before which the most brilliant achievements of the learned, the wise, and the experienced have paled.

9.21 Particular attention, I feel, should, at this juncture, be directed to the various Indian tribes, the aboriginal inhabitants of the Latin republics, whom the Author of the Tablets of the Divine Plan has compared to the "ancient inhabitants of the Arabian Peninsula." "Attach great importance," is His admonition to the entire body of the believers in the United States and the Dominion of Canada, "to the indigenous population of America. For these souls may be likened unto the ancient inhabitants of the Arabian Peninsula, who, prior to the Mission of Muhammad, were like unto savages. When the light of Muhammad shone forth in their midst, however, they became so radiant as to illumine the world. Likewise, these Indians, should they be educated and guided, there can be no doubt that they will become so illumined as to enlighten the whole world." The initial contact already established, in the concluding years of the first Bahá'í century, in obedience to 'Abdu'l-Bahá's Mandate, with the Cherokee and Oneida Indians in North Carolina and Wisconsin, with the Patagonian, the Mexican and the Inca Indians, and the Mayans in Argentina, Mexico, Peru and Yucatan, respectively, should, as the Latin American Bahá'í communities gain in stature and strength, be consolidated and extended. A special effort should be exerted to secure the unqualified adherence of members of some of these tribes to the Faith, their subsequent election to its councils, and their unreserved support of the organized attempts that will have to be made in the future by the projected national assemblies for the large-scale conversion of Indian races to the Faith of Bahá'u'lláh.

9.22 People are so markedly lacking in spirituality these days that the Bahá'ís should consciously guard themselves against being caught in what one might call the undertow of materialism and atheism, sweeping the world these days. Skepticism, cynicism, disbelief, immorality and hard-heartedness are rife, and as friends are those who stand for the antithesis of all these things they should beware lest the atmosphere of the present world affects them without their being conscious of it.

9.23 He has emphasized on more than one occasion that the important thing for the pioneer to do is to bend his energies toward teaching the native people of the country. He should teach and confirm them, and assist them to gradually shoulder their responsibilities in the Faith and become the active supporters and upholders of its institutions. This means that the Cause then is built on a solid foundation, and is not being carried forward by people who have gone to that country from other lands. Then too, in most people there is a certain degree of hidden feeling of racial distinction, whether or not they realize or admit it; and those other than natives may be called upon to experience great tests upon accepting the Faith, because of its principle of complete freedom from prejudice.

This does not mean that people other than natives are not to be taught, if you find they are really spiritually prepared for the Message of Bahá'u'lláh; but the important thing is to strive to teach and confirm a few native people, who will not only themselves become quickened with its spirit, but who will in turn, like Enoch Olinga from Uganda, quickly ignite the flame of the Faith in the hearts of others of their countrymen.

9.24 It is a great mistake to believe that because people are illiterate or live primitive lives, they are lacking in either intelligence or sensibility. On the contrary, they may well look on us with the evils of our civilization, with its moral corruption, its ruinous wars, its hypocrisy and conceit, as people who merit watching with both suspicion and contempt. We should meet them as equals, well-wishers, people who admire and respect their ancient decent, and who feel that they will be interested as we are in a living religion and not in the dead forms of present-day churches.

9.25 Shoghi Effendi is also most anxious for the Message to reach the aboriginal inhabitants of the Americas. These people for the most part downtrodden and ignorant should receive from the Bahá'ís special measure of love, and every effort be made to teach them. Their enrollment in the Faith will enrich them and us and demonstrate our principle of the Oneness of Man far better than words or the wide conversion of the ruling races ever can.

9.26 The original population of the United States was very dear to 'Abdu'l-Bahá's heart, and He foretold for the Indians a great future if they accepted and became enlightened by the Teachings of Bahá'u'lláh.

To believe in the Mouthpiece of God in His Day confers very great blessings, not only on individuals, but on races, and He hopes that you who are now numbered amongst the followers of Bahá'u'lláh will give His Message to many more of your tribe, and in this way hasten for your people a bright and happy future.

FROM THE WRITINGS AND LETTERS WRITTEN BY, OR ON BEHALF OF, THE UNIVERSAL HOUSE OF JUSTICE

9.27 Many are the goals which now challenge the peoples of the North under the Five Year Plan: encouraging and educating the children and stimulating and guiding the youth; a wider participation of women in Bahá'í services; a greater assumption by the indigenous inhabitants of these regions of responsibilities in the leadership and administration of the community; a bolder proclamation of the Faith by radio and television; and a more far-flung and intensified campaign of teaching, audaciously conceived by National Spiritual Assemblies and their agencies and vigorously executed by Local Spiritual Assemblies and individual believers, aiming at a vast increase in the number of adherents to the Faith from every segment of society, a multiplication of Baháʾí administrative institutions, and a richer and more diverse range of publications in all media. What will set the seal on the success of the Plan and pave the way for the long-awaited and divinely promised glories of the future, is a mightier effort by every supporter of the Most Great Name in those climes to increasingly deepen themselves in the teachings, to pour forth their substance in the path of His love, to resolve to conform their personal lives to the high standards set in His teachings, and to undertake more daring tasks however great the sacrifice, and more extensive travels however arduous the voyage. In this wise will they draw nearer to the Spirit of Baháʾuʾlláh and become true and radiant signs of His Most Great Guidance. These are the tasks! This is the work!

9.28   We pray at the Sacred Threshold that the Baháʾís of the North may in the not- too-distant future transform the Arctic into that spiritual rose garden and heavenly paradise longed and yearned for by ʿAbduʾl-Bahá, and that its peoples may be bountifully blessed and lovingly guided in their selfless services to promote the Faith of Baháʾuʾlláh

9.29   We direct a special appeal to the indigenous believers in all parts of the Pacific region, men and women alike, to intensify their efforts to acquire a deeper understanding of the Revelation of Baháʾuʾlláh, and to strive for a position in the forefront of the promoters of the Faith through their teaching endeavours on the home front and their international cooperation in programmes of the Ocean of Light. As the tensions and divisions of a declining social order increase, the believers throughout the Pacific Islands should provide compelling testimony to the potency of the Baháʾí Teachings through their manifest unity transcending tribal, national or ethnic barriers. The desperate search for solutions to the social and economic problems afflicting these countries is tempting people, in increasing numbers, to indulge in partisan political activities; the indigenous Bahá'ís should refuse to be drawn into such divisive pursuits and should strive to acquire a more profound insight into the nature of the World Order of Bahá'u'lláh, which offers a pattern for a future society distinguished by justice and unity, far removed from the contention of competing political interests.

9.30 In the Divine Plan bequeathed to you by 'Abdu'l-Bahá is disclosed the glorious destiny of those who are the descendants of the early inhabitants of your continent. We call upon the indigenous believers who are firmly rooted in the Bahá'í Teachings to aid, through both deed and word, those who have not yet attained that level of understanding. Progress along the path to their destiny requires that they refuse to be drawn into the divisiveness and militancy around them, and that they strive to make their own distinctive contribution to the pursuit of the goals of the Four Year Plan, both beyond the confines of North America and at home. They should be ever mindful of the vital contribution they can make to the work of the Faith throughout the American continent, in the circumpolar areas and in the Asian region of the Russian Federation.

OTHER SOURCES

9.31 At the outset, we believe that any declaration on the rights of indigenous peoples must emphasize four main principles: one, respect for indigenous communities and their cultures; two, appreciation for cultural diversity; three, full participation of indigenous peoples; and four, co-operation between indigenous peoples and their governments.

Firstly, a declaration should insist that indigenous peoples have the right to maintain and develop their unique cultures and ways of life. The declaration must, of course, condemn outright genocide, legally-sanctioned discrimination, and other direct forms of oppression. But it should also call for efforts aimed at erasing more subtle forms of discrimination and prejudice directed towards indigenous peoples.

Secondly, cultural diversity: Indigenous peoples have suffered terrible oppression because new settlers did not tolerate diversity, but viewed their own cultures as superior and more advanced. Appreciation for diverse cultures and ethnic characteristics is, in the Bahá'í view, a prerequisite for the elimination of discrimination against indigenous populations. We are convinced, therefore, that a declaration should call for educational measures that seek to foster an awareness of, and appreciation for, cultural diversity. All people — indigenous peoples as well as members of other cultures — should have the opportunity to benefit from mind-broadening educational programmes designed to increase understanding between indigenous peoples and the dominant society, as well as between different groups of the indigenous peoples themselves. For these reasons, we welcome preliminary draft principle 11, adopted by the Working Group at its last session, affirming the right of indigenous peoples "to promote intercultural information and education, recognizing the dignity and diversity of their cultures."

Thirdly, indigenous peoples must have the right to participate fully and actively in their national societies and in decisions that affect them. Their participation will enrich the lives of their national communities. More importantly, it will allow them to guide their own destinies. Full and active participation will enable indigenous peoples to develop the confidence, self-reliance and leadership skills that are essential if they are to play an active part in providing a higher level of social, economic and spiritual well-being for their peoples. It will permit them to become fully-contributing members of their national communities, while simultaneously preserving their unique cultures and identities. A declaration must call for measures to promote the development of opportunities for such active participation of indigenous peoples.

Fourthly and finally, cooperation between indigenous peoples and their governments is essential. In the Bahá'í view, respect for different cultures can only be achieved if we are able to perceive, underlying our cultural variations, our essential unity as one human race. Mutual respect will not come about through separatism or antagonism. Indigenous peoples feel understandable anger at the injustices they have experienced. But the amelioration of their current situation requires a new dialogue between indigenous peoples and their government—positive communication aimed at finding ways to promote indigenous rights and participation. A declaration should call for such co-operation. It should advocate the creation of a permanent mechanism—perhaps an ombudsman or a successor to this Working Group—to bring indigenous peoples and their governments together on a regular basis so that they can air problems and perspectives and discuss remedies and solutions in a constructive manner. (Bahá'í International Community, 1988 Aug 01, *Rights of Indigenous Populations*)

CHAPTER 10:

PATHS FROM AGNOSTICISM TO THE BAHÁ'Í FAITH

FROM THE WRITINGS OF BAHÁ'U'LLÁH

10.1 We have decreed, O people, that the highest and last end of all learning be the recognition of Him Who is the Object of all knowledge; and yet, behold how ye have allowed your learning to shut you out, as by a veil, from Him Who is the Dayspring of this Light, through Whom every hidden thing hath been revealed. Could ye but discover the source whence the splendour of this utterance is diffused, ye would cast away the peoples of the world and all that they possess, and would draw nigh unto this most blessed Seat of glory.

10.2 To every discerning and illuminated heart it is evident that God, the unknowable Essence, the Divine Being, is immensely exalted beyond every human attribute, such as corporeal existence, ascent and descent, egress and regress. Far be it from His glory that human tongue should adequately recount His praise, or that human heart comprehend His fathomless mystery. He is, and hath ever been, veiled in the ancient eternity of His Essence, and will remain in His Reality everlastingly hidden from the sight of men.

10.3 The door of the knowledge of the Ancient Being hath ever been, and will continue for ever to be, closed in the face of men. No man's understanding shall ever gain access unto His holy court. As a token of His mercy, however, and as a proof of His loving-kindness, He hath manifested unto men the Day Stars of His divine guidance, the Symbols of His divine unity, and hath ordained the knowledge of these sanctified Beings to be identical with the knowledge of His own Self. Whoso recognizeth them hath recognized God. Whoso hearkeneth to their call, hath hearkened to the Voice of God, and whoso testifieth to the truth of their Revelation, hath testified to the truth of God Himself. Whoso turneth away from them, hath turned away from God, and whoso disbelieveth in them, hath disbelieved in God. Every one of them is the Way of God that connecteth this world with the realms above, and the Standard of His Truth unto every one in the kingdoms of earth and heaven. They are the Manifestations of God amidst men, the evidences of His Truth, and the signs of His glory.

10.4 If ye believe, to your own behoof will ye believe; and if ye believe not, ye yourselves will suffer

10.5 Say: Nature in its essence is the embodiment of My Name, the Maker, the Creator. Its manifestations are diversified by varying causes, and in this diversity there are signs for men of discernment. Nature is God's Will and is its expression in and through the contingent world. It is a dispensation of Providence ordained by the Ordainer, the All-Wise. Were anyone to affirm that it is the Will of God as manifested in the world of being, no one should question this assertion. It is endowed with a power whose reality men of learning fail to grasp. Indeed a man of insight can perceive naught therein save the effulgent splendour of Our Name, the Creator. Say: This is an existence which knoweth no decay, and Nature itself is lost in bewilderment before its revelations, its compelling evidences and its effulgent glory which have encompassed the universe.

10.6 The essence and the fundamentals of philosophy have emanated from the Prophets. That the people differ concerning the inner meanings and mysteries thereof is to be attributed to the divergence of their views and minds. We would fain recount to thee the following: One of the Prophets once was communicating to his people that with which the Omnipotent Lord had inspired Him. Truly, thy Lord is the Inspirer, the Gracious, the Exalted. When the fountain of wisdom and eloquence gushed forth from the wellspring of His utterance and the wine of divine knowledge inebriated those who had sought His threshold, He exclaimed: 'Lo! All are filled with the Spirit.' From among the people there was he who held fast unto this statement and, actuated by his own fancies, conceived the idea that the spirit literally penetrateth or entereth into the body, and through lengthy expositions he advanced proofs to vindicate this concept; and groups of people followed in his footsteps. To mention their names at this point, or to give thee a detailed account thereof, would lead to prolixity, and would depart from the main theme. Verily, thy Lord is the All-Wise, the All-Knowing. There was also he who partook of the choice wine whose seal had been removed by the Key of the Tongue of Him Who is the Revealer of the Verses of thy Lord, the Gracious, the Most Generous.

10.7 After Socrates came the divine Plato who was a pupil of the former and occupied the chair of philosophy as his successor. He acknowledged his belief in God and in His signs which pervade all that hath been and shall be. Then came Aristotle, the well-known man of knowledge. He it is who discovered the power of gaseous matter. These men who stand out as leaders of the people and are pre-eminent among them, one and all acknowledged their belief in the immortal Being Who holdeth in His grasp the reins of all sciences.

10.8 The Great Being saith: The learned of the day must direct the people to acquire those branches of knowledge which are of use, that both the learned themselves and the generality of mankind may derive benefits therefrom. Such academic pursuits as begin and end in words alone have never been and will never be of any worth. The majority of Persia's learned doctors devote all their lives to the study of a philosophy the ultimate yield of which is nothing but words.

10.9 It is incumbent upon them who are in authority to exercise moderation in all things. Whatsoever passeth beyond the limits of moderation will cease to exert a beneficial influence. Consider for instance such things as liberty, civilization and the like. However much men of understanding may favourably regard them, they will, if carried to excess, exercise a pernicious influence upon men.

10.10 Whoso cleaveth to justice, can, under no circumstances, transgress the limits of moderation. He discerneth the truth in all things, through the guidance of Him Who is the All-Seeing. The civilization, so often vaunted by the learned exponents of arts and sciences, will, if allowed to overleap the bounds of moderation, bring great evil upon men. Thus warneth you He Who is the All-Knowing. If carried to excess, civilization will prove as prolific a source of evil as it had been of goodness when kept within the restraints of moderation. Meditate on this, O people, and be not of them that wander distraught in the wilderness of error. The day is approaching when its flame will devour the cities, when the Tongue of Grandeur will proclaim: "The Kingdom is God's, the Almighty, the All-Praised!"

10.11 Notwithstanding the divinely-inspired admonitions of all the Prophets, the Saints, and Chosen ones of God, enjoining the people to see with their own eyes and hear with their own ears, they have disdainfully rejected their counsels and have blindly followed, and will continue to follow, the leaders of their Faith.

10.12 Know ye that the embodiment of liberty and its symbol is the animal. That which beseemeth man is submission unto such restraints as will protect him from his own ignorance, and guard him against the harm of the mischief-maker. Liberty causeth man to overstep the bounds of propriety, and to infringe on the dignity of his station. It debaseth him to the level of extreme depravity and wickedness.

Regard men as a flock of sheep that need a shepherd for their protection. This, verily, is the truth, the certain truth. We approve of liberty in certain circumstances, and refuse to sanction it in others. We, verily, are the All-Knowing.

Say: True liberty consisteth in man's submission unto My commandments, little as ye know it.

10.13 It is permissible to study sciences and arts, but such sciences as are useful and would redound to the progress and advancement of the people. Thus hath it been decreed by Him Who is the Ordainer, the All-Wise

FROM THE WRITINGS AND UTTERANCES OF 'ABDU'L-BAHÁ

10.14 Thou hast described thyself as a student in the school of spiritual progress. Fortunate art thou! If these schools of progress lead to the university of heaven, then branches of knowledge will be developed whereby humanity will look upon the tablet of existence as a scroll endlessly unfolding; and all created things will be seen upon that scroll as letters and words. Then will the different planes of meaning be learned, and then within every atom of the universe will be witnessed the signs of the oneness of God.

Chapter 10: Paths from Agnosticism to the Bahá'í Faith 131

10.15 In short, man is endowed with two natures: one tendeth towards moral sublimity and intellectual perfection, while the other turneth to bestial degradation and carnal imperfections. If ye travel the countries of the globe ye shall observe on one side the remains of ruin and destruction, while on the other ye shall see the signs of civilization and development. Such desolation and ruin are the result of war, strife and quarrelling, while all development and progress are fruits of the lights of virtue, co-operation and concord.

10.16 Throughout the world of existence it is the same; the smallest created thing proves that there is a creator. For instance, this piece of bread proves that it has a maker.

10.17 And among the teachings of Bahá'u'lláh is that religion is a mighty bulwark. If the edifice of religion shakes and totters, commotion and chaos will ensue and the order of things will be utterly upset, for in the world of mankind there are two safeguards that protect man from wrongdoing. One is the law which punishes the criminal; but the law prevents only the manifest crime and not the concealed sin; whereas the ideal safeguard, namely, the religion of God, prevents both the manifest and the concealed crime, trains man, educates morals, compels the adoption of virtues and is the all-inclusive power which guarantees the felicity of the world of mankind. But by religion is meant that which is ascertained by investigation and not that which is based on mere imitation, the foundations of Divine Religions and not human imitations.

10.18 And among the teachings of Bahá'u'lláh is the promotion of education. Every child must be instructed in sciences as much as is necessary. If the parents are able to provide the expenses of this education, it is well, otherwise the community must provide the means for the teaching of that child.

10.19 This people, all of them, have pictured a god in the realm of the mind, and worship that image which they have made for themselves. And yet that image is comprehended, the human mind being the comprehender thereof, and certainly the comprehender is greater than that which lieth within its grasp;

for imagination is but the branch, while mind is the root; and certainly the root is greater than the branch. Consider then, how all the peoples of the world are bowing the knee to a fancy of their own contriving, how they have created a creator within their own minds, and they call it the Fashioner of all that is—whereas in truth it is but an illusion. Thus are the people worshipping only an error of perception.

But that Essence of Essences, that Invisible of Invisibles, is sanctified above all human speculation, and never to be overtaken by the mind of man. Never shall that immemorial Reality lodge within the compass of a contingent being. His is another realm, and of that realm no understanding can be won. No access can be gained thereto; all entry is forbidden there. The utmost one can say is that Its existence can be proved, but the conditions of Its existence are unknown.

10.20 Also, most of the miracles of the Prophets which are mentioned have an inner significance. For instance, in the Gospel it is written that at the martyrdom of Christ darkness prevailed, and the earth quaked, and the veil of the Temple was rent in twain from the top to the bottom, and the dead came forth from their graves. If these events had happened, they would indeed have been awesome, and would certainly have been recorded in the history of the times. They would have become the cause of much troublings of heart. Either the soldiers would have taken down Christ from the cross, or they would have fled. These events are not related in any history; therefore, it is evident they ought not to be taken literally, but as having an inner significance.

Our purpose is not to deny such miracles; our only meaning is that they do not constitute decisive proofs, and that they have an inner significance.

10.21 The outward miracles have no importance for the people of Reality. If a blind man receives sight, for example, he will finally again become sightless, for he will die and be deprived of all his senses and powers. Therefore, causing the blind man to see is comparatively of little importance, for this faculty of sight will at last disappear. If the body of a dead person be resuscitated, of what use is it since the body will die again?

Chapter 10: Paths from Agnosticism to the Bahá'í Faith 133

> But it is important to give perception and eternal life—that is, the spiritual and divine life. For this physical life is not immortal, and its existence is equivalent to nonexistence. So it is that Christ said to one of His disciples: "Let the dead bury their dead;" for "That which is born of the flesh is flesh; and that which is born of the Spirit is spirit."[1]
> [1 Matt. 8:22; John 3:6.]

10.22 If reason is the perfect standard and criterion of knowledge, why are opinions at variance and why do philosophers disagree so completely with each other? This is a clear proof that human reason is not to be relied upon as an infallible criterion. For instance, great discoveries and announcements of former centuries are continually upset and discarded by the wise men of today. Mathematicians, astronomers, chemical scientists continually disprove and reject the conclusions of the ancients; nothing is fixed, nothing final; everything is continually changing because human reason is progressing along new roads of investigation and arriving at new conclusions every day. In the future much that is announced and accepted as true now will be rejected and disproved. And so it will continue ad infinitum.

10.23 Material virtues have attained great development, but ideal virtues have been left far behind. If you should ask a thousand persons, "What are the proofs of the reality of Divinity?" perhaps not one would be able to answer. If you should ask further, "What proofs have you regarding the essence of God?" "How do you explain inspiration and revelation?" "What are the evidences of conscious intelligence beyond the material universe?" "Can you suggest a plan and method for the betterment of human moralities?" "Can you clearly define and differentiate the world of nature and the world of Divinity?"—you would receive very little real knowledge and enlightenment upon these questions. This is due to the fact that development of the ideal virtues has been neglected. People speak of Divinity, but the ideas and beliefs they have of Divinity are, in reality, superstition. Divinity is the effulgence of the Sun of Reality, the manifestation of spiritual virtues and ideal powers. The intellectual proofs of Divinity are based upon observation and evidence which constitute decisive argument, logically proving the reality of Divinity, the effulgence of mercy, the certainty of inspiration and immortality of the spirit. This is, in reality, the science of Divinity. Divinity is not what is set forth in dogmas and sermons of the church. Ordinarily when the word Divinity is mentioned, it is associated in the minds of the hearers with certain formulas and doctrines, whereas it essentially means the wisdom and knowledge of God, the effulgence of the Sun of Truth, the revelation of reality and divine philosophy.

10.24 The imperfect members of society, the weak souls in humanity, follow their natural trend. Their lives and actions are in accord with their natural propensities; they are captives of physical susceptibilities; they are not in touch or in tune with the spiritual bounties. Man has two aspects: the physical, which is subject to nature, and the merciful or divine, which is connected with God. If the physical or natural disposition in him should overcome the heavenly and merciful, he is, then, the most degraded of animal beings; and if the divine and spiritual should triumph over the human and natural, he is, verily, an angel. The Prophets come into the world to guide and educate humanity so that the animal nature of man may disappear and the divinity of his powers become awakened. The divine aspect or spiritual nature consists of the breaths of the Holy Spirit. The second birth of which Jesus has spoken refers to the appearance of this heavenly nature in man. It is expressed in the baptism of the Holy Spirit, and he who is baptized by the Holy Spirit is a veritable manifestation of divine mercy to mankind. Then he becomes just and kind to all humanity; he entertains prejudice and ill will toward none; he shuns no nation or people.

10.25 Furthermore, know ye that God has created in man the power of reason, whereby man is enabled to investigate reality. God has not intended man to imitate blindly his fathers and ancestors. He has endowed him with mind, or the faculty of reasoning, by the exercise of which he is to investigate and discover the truth, and that which he finds real and true he must accept. He must not be an imitator or blind follower of any soul. He must not rely implicitly upon the opinion of any man without investigation; nay, each soul must seek intelligently and independently, arriving at a real conclusion and bound only by that reality. The greatest cause of bereavement and disheartening in the world of humanity is ignorance based upon blind imitation. It is due to this that wars and battles prevail; from this cause hatred and animosity arise continually among mankind. Through failure to investigate reality the Jews rejected Jesus Christ. They were expecting His coming; by day and night they mourned and lamented, saying, "O God! Hasten Thou the day of the advent of Christ," expressing most intense longing for the Messiah; but when Christ appeared, they denied and rejected Him, treated Him with arrogant contempt, sentenced Him to death and finally crucified Him. Why did this happen? Because they were blindly following imitations, believing that which had descended to them as a heritage from their fathers and ancestors, tenaciously holding to it and refusing to investigate the reality of Christ. Therefore, they were deprived of the bounties of Christ, whereas if they had forsaken imitations and investigated the reality of the Messiah, they would have surely been guided to believing in Him. Instead of this they said, "We have heard from our fathers and have read in the Old Testament that Christ must come from an unknown place; now we find that this one has come from Nazareth." Steeped in the literal interpretation and imitating the beliefs of fathers and ancestors, they failed to understand the fact that although the body of Jesus came from Nazareth, the reality of the Christ came from the unknown place of the divine Kingdom. They also said that the scepter of Christ would be of iron—that is to say, He should wield a sword. When Christ appeared, He did possess a sword; but it was the sword of His tongue with which He separated the false from the true. But the Jews were blind to the spiritual significance and symbolism of the prophetic words. They also expected that the Messiah would sit upon the throne of David, whereas Christ had neither throne nor semblance of sovereignty; nay, rather, He was a poor man, apparently abject and vanquished; therefore, how could He be the veritable Christ? This was one of their most insistent objections based upon ancestral interpretation and teaching. In reality, Christ was glorified with an eternal sovereignty and everlasting dominion—spiritual and not temporal. His throne and Kingdom were established in human hearts, where He reigns with power and authority without end. Notwithstanding the fulfillment of all the prophetic signs in Christ, the Jews denied Him and entered the period of their deprivation because of their allegiance to imitations and ancestral forms.

10.26 Another new principle revealed by Bahá'u'lláh is the injunction to investigate truth—that is to say, no man should blindly follow his ancestors and forefathers. Nay, each must see with his own eyes, hear with his own ears and investigate the truth himself in order that he may follow the truth instead of blind acquiescence and imitation of ancestral beliefs.

10.27 All down the ages we see how blood has stained the surface of the earth; but now a ray of greater light has come, man's intelligence is greater, spirituality is beginning to grow, and a time is surely coming when the religions of the world will be at peace. Let us leave the discordant arguments concerning outward forms, and let us join together to hasten forward the Divine Cause of unity, until all humanity knows itself to be one family, joined together in love.

10.28 This is a new cycle of human power. All the horizons of the world are luminous, and the world will become indeed as a garden and a paradise. It is the hour of unity of the sons of men and of the drawing together of all races and all classes. You are loosed from ancient superstitions which have kept men ignorant, destroying the foundation of true humanity.

10.29 Religion and Science are inter-twined with each other and cannot be separated. These are the two wings with which humanity must fly. One wing is not enough. Every religion which does not concern itself with Science is mere tradition, and that is not the essential. Therefore science, education and civilization are most important necessities for the full religious life.

10.30 Divine things are too deep to be expressed by common words. The heavenly teachings are expressed in parable in order to be understood and preserved for ages to come. When the spiritually minded dive deeply into the ocean of their meaning they bring to the surface the pearls of their inner significance. There is no greater pleasure than to study God's Word with a spiritual mind.

10.31 Bahá'u'lláh taught, that Religion is the chief foundation of Love and Unity and the cause of Oneness. If a religion become the cause of hatred and disharmony, it would be better that it should not exist. To be without such a religion is better than to be with it.

10.32 In proclaiming the oneness of mankind He taught that men and women are equal in the sight of God and that there is no distinction to be made between them. The only difference between them now is due to lack of education and training. If woman is given equal opportunity of education, distinction and estimate of inferiority will disappear. The world of humanity has two wings, as it were: One is the female; the other is the male. If one wing be defective, the strong perfect wing will not be capable of flight

FROM THE WRITINGS AND LETTERS WRITTEN BY, OR ON BEHALF OF, SHOGHI EFFENDI

10.33 People are so markedly lacking in spirituality these days that the Bahá'ís should consciously guard themselves against being caught in what one might call the undertow of materialism and atheism, sweeping the world these days. Skepticism, cynicism, disbelief, immorality and hard-heartedness are rife, and as friends are those who stand for the antithesis of all these things they should beware lest the atmosphere of the present world affects them without their being conscious of it.

10.34 Just as in the past the Prophets have been persecuted and their Mission was ridiculed, so has the Message of Bahá'u'lláh been scoffed at as a mere impractical idealism. From His earliest youth He was put in chains, expatriated and persecuted. But what do we observe in this Day?...the principles He advocated are the only solution for practical politics, the spiritual truths He voiced are the crying needs of man and the very things he requires for his moral and spiritual development.

He does not ask us to follow Him blindly; as He says in one of His Tablets, God has endowed man with a mind to operate as a torchlight and guide him to the truth. Read His words, consider His Teachings and measure their value in the light of contemporary problems and the truth will surely be revealed to you. Read books such as the Íqán, Some Answered Questions, Nabíl's Narrative, and you will appreciate the truth of His Mission, as well as the true spirit He creates in whosoever follows His ways.

10.35 Indeed, the chief reason for the evils now rampant in society is the lack of spirituality. The materialistic civilization of our age has so much absorbed the energy and interest of mankind that people in general do no longer feel the necessity of raising themselves above the forces and conditions of their daily material existence. There is not sufficient demand for things that we should call spiritual to differentiate them from the needs and requirements of our physical existence.

The universal crisis affecting mankind is, therefore, essentially spiritual in its causes. The spirit of the age, taken on the whole, is irreligious. Man's outlook on life is too crude and materialistic to enable him to elevate himself into the higher realms of the spirit.

It is this condition, so sadly morbid, into which society has fallen, that religion seeks to improve and transform...

10.36 ... The academic life also has its fashions and fads, even though they are of a different nature from the fads of the man on the street. "These fashions are not permanent they are bound to change. Today the fad is a materialistic view of life and of the world. A day will soon come when it will become deeply religious and spiritual. In fact, we can discern the beginning of such a change in the writings of some of the most eminent souls and liberal minds. When the pendulum will start its full swing then we shall see all such eminent men turn again to God.

10.37 ... How to attain spirituality is indeed a question to which every young man and woman must sooner or later try to find a satisfactory answer. It is precisely because no such satisfactory answer has been given or found, that the modern youth finds itself bewildered, and is being consequently, carried away by the materialistic forces that are so powerfully undermining the foundations of man's moral and spiritual life ... It is this condition so sadly morbid, into which society has fallen, that religion seeks to improve and transform. "For the core of religious faith is that mystic feeling which unites man with God. This state of spiritual communion can be brought about and maintained by means of meditation and prayer. And this is the reason why Bahá'u'lláh has so much stressed the importance of worship.

It is not sufficient for a believer merely to accept and observe the teachings. He should, in addition, cultivate the sense of spirituality which he can acquire chiefly by means of prayer...

The believers, particularly the young ones, should therefore fully realize the necessity of praying. For prayer is absolutely indispensable to their inner spiritual development, and this, as already stated, is the very foundation and purpose of the religion of God.

FROM THE WRITINGS AND LETTERS WRITTEN BY, OR ON BEHALF OF, THE UNIVERSAL HOUSE OF JUSTICE

10.38   In the midst of a civilization torn by strifes and enfeebled by materialism, the people of Baha are building a new world. We face at this time opportunities and responsibilities of vast magnitude and great urgency. Let each believer in his inmost heart resolve not to be seduced by the ephemeral allurements of the society around him, nor to be drawn into its feuds and short-lived enthusiasms, but instead to transfer all he can from the old world to that new one which is the vision of his longing and will be the fruit of his labours.

10.39   The proper education of children is of vital importance to the progress of mankind, and the heart and essential foundation of all education is spiritual and moral training. When we teach our fellowmen the truths and way of life of the Bahá'í Faith we have to struggle against barriers of indifference, materialism, superstition and a multitude of erroneous preconceptions; but in our new-born children we are presented with pure souls, untarnished by the world. As they grow they will face countless tests and difficulties. From their earliest moments we have the duty to train them, both spiritually and materially, in the way that God has shown, and thus, as they come to adulthood, they can become champions of His Cause and spiritual and moral giants among mankind, equipped to meet all tests, and will be, indeed, "stars of the heaven of understanding," "soft-flowing waters upon which must depend the very life of all men."

10.40 Undoubtedly the fact that Bahá'í scholars of the history and teachings of the Faith believe in the Faith that they are studying will be a grave flaw in the eyes of many non-Bahá'í academics, whose own dogmatic materialism passes without comment because it is fashionable; but this difficulty is one that Bahá'í scholars share with their fellow believers in many fields of human endeavour.

10.41 These are momentous times. The institutions of the old world order are crumbling and in disarray. Materialism, greed, corruption and conflict are infecting the social order with a grave malaise from which it is helpless to extricate itself. With every passing day it becomes more and more evident that no time must be lost in applying the remedy prescribed by Bahá'u'lláh, and it is to this task that Bahá'ís everywhere must bend their energies and commit their resources.

10.42 This turning away from religion has been powerfully reinforced by the growth of materialism, and has produced a combination of physical well-being and spiritual aridity that is having catastrophic results, socially and psychologically, on the population.

10.43 The time has come when those who preach the dogmas of materialism, whether of the east or the west, whether of capitalism or socialism, must give account of the moral stewardship they have presumed to exercise. Where is the "new world" promised by these ideologies? Where is the international peace to whose ideals they proclaim their devotion?

Chapter 10: Paths from Agnosticism to the Bahá'í Faith 141

Where are the breakthroughs into new realms of cultural achievement produced by the aggrandizement of this race, of that nation or of a particular class? Why is the vast majority of the world's peoples sinking ever deeper into hunger and wretchedness when wealth on a scale undreamed of by the Pharaohs, the Caesars, or even the imperialist powers of the nineteenth century is at the disposal of the present arbiters of human affairs?

Most particularly, it is in the glorification of material pursuits, at once the progenitor and common feature of all such ideologies, that we find the roots which nourish the falsehood that human beings are incorrigibly selfish and aggressive. It is here that the ground must be cleared for the building of a new world fit for our descendants.

That materialistic ideals have, in the light of experience, failed to satisfy the needs of mankind calls for an honest acknowledgement that a fresh effort must now be made to find the solutions to the agonizing problems of the planet. The intolerable conditions pervading society bespeak a common failure of all, a circumstance which tends to incite rather than relieve the entrenchment on every side. Clearly, a common remedial effort is urgently required. It is primarily a matter of attitude. Will humanity continue in its waywardness, holding to outworn concepts and unworkable assumptions? Or will its leaders, regardless of ideology, step forth and, with a resolute will, consult together in a united search for appropriate solutions?

Those who care for the future of the human race may well ponder this advice. "If long-cherished ideals and time-honoured institutions, if certain social assumptions and religious formulae have ceased to promote the welfare of the generality of mankind, if they no longer minister to the needs of a continually evolving humanity, let them be swept away and relegated to the limbo of obsolescent and forgotten doctrines. Why should these, in a world subject to the immutable law of change and decay, be exempt from the deterioration that must needs overtake every human institution? For legal standards, political and economic theories are solely designed to safeguard the interests of humanity as a whole, and not humanity to be crucified for the preservation of the integrity of any particular law or doctrine."

OTHER SOURCES

10.44 The assumptions directing most of current development planning are essentially materialistic. That is to say, the purpose of development is defined in terms of the successful cultivation in all societies of those means for the achievement of material prosperity that have, through trial and error, already come to characterize certain regions of the world. Modifications in development discourse do indeed occur, accommodating differences of culture and political system and responding to the alarming dangers posed by environmental degradation. Yet the underlying materialistic assumptions remain essentially unchallenged.

As the twentieth century draws to a close, it is no longer possible to maintain the belief that the approach to social and economic development to which the materialistic conception of life has given rise is capable of meeting humanity's needs. Optimistic forecasts about the changes it would generate have vanished into the ever-widening abyss that separates the living standards of a small and relatively diminishing minority of the world's inhabitants from the poverty experienced by the vast majority of the globe's population.

This unprecedented economic crisis, together with the social breakdown it has helped to engender, reflects a profound error of conception about human nature itself. For the levels of response elicited from human beings by the incentives of the prevailing order are not only inadequate, but seem almost irrelevant in the face of world events. We are being shown that, unless the development of society finds a purpose beyond the mere amelioration of material conditions, it will fail of attaining even these goals. That purpose must be sought in spiritual dimensions of life and motivation that transcend a constantly changing economic landscape and an artificially imposed division of human societies into "developed" and "developing".

As the purpose of development is being redefined, it will become necessary also to look again at assumptions about the appropriate roles to be played by the protagonists in the process. The crucial role of government, at whatever level, requires no elaboration. Future generations, however, will find almost incomprehensible the circumstance that, in an age paying tribute to an egalitarian philosophy and related democratic principles, development planning should view the masses of humanity as essentially recipients of benefits from aid and training. Despite acknowledgement of participation as a principle, the scope of the decision-making left to most of the world's population is at best secondary, limited to a range of choices formulated by agencies inaccessible to them and determined by goals that are often irreconcilable with their perceptions of reality.

This approach is even endorsed, implicitly if not explicitly, by established religion. Burdened by traditions of paternalism, prevailing religious thought seems incapable of translating an expressed faith in the spiritual dimensions of human nature into confidence in humanity's collective capacity to transcend material conditions. (Bahá'í International Community, 1995 Mar 03, *The Prosperity of Humankind*)

10.45 Indeed, the unifying effect of the twentieth century revolution is nowhere more readily apparent than in the implications of the changes that took place in scientific and technological life. At the most obvious level, the human race is now endowed with the means needed to realize the visionary goals summoned up by a steadily maturing consciousness. Viewed more deeply, this empowerment is potentially available to all of the earth's inhabitants, without regard to race, culture, or nation. "A new life", Bahá'u'lláh prophetically saw, "is, in this age, stirring within all the peoples of the earth; and yet none hath discovered its cause or perceived its motive." Today, more than a century after these words were written, the implications of what has since taken place begin to be apparent to thoughtful minds everywhere.(Bahá'í International Community, 1999 Feb, *Who is Writing the Future*)

10.46 No aspect of contemporary civilization is more directly challenged by Bahá'u'lláh's conception of the future than is the prevailing cult of individualism, which has spread to most parts of the world. Nurtured by such cultural forces as political ideology, academic elitism, and a consumer economy, the "pursuit of happiness" has given rise to an aggressive and almost boundless sense of personal entitlement. The moral consequences have been corrosive for the individual and society alike - and devastating in terms of disease, drug addiction and other all-too-familiar blights of century's end. The task of freeing humanity from an error so fundamental and pervasive will call into question some of the twentieth century's most deeply entrenched assumptions about right and wrong. (Bahá'í International Community, 1999 Feb, *Who is Writing the Future*)

10.47 Spiritual and materialistic conceptions of the nature of reality are irreconcilable with one another and lead in opposite directions. As a new century opens, the course set by the second of these two opposing views has already carried a hapless humanity far beyond the outermost point where an illusion of rationality, let alone of human well-being, could once be sustained. With every passing day, the signs multiply that great numbers of people everywhere are awakening to this realization. (Bahá'í International Community, 1999 Feb, *Who is Writing the Future*)

PART III: NEXT STEPS

CHAPTER 11:

MANY DESTINATIONS FOR MANY PATHS

FROM THE WRITINGS OF BAHÁ'U'LLÁH

11.1   O people! Consort with the followers of all religions in a spirit of friendliness and fellowship.

11.2   O My servants! Deprive not yourselves of the unfading and resplendent Light that shineth within the Lamp of Divine glory. Let the flame of the love of God burn brightly within your radiant hearts. Feed it with the oil of Divine guidance, and protect it within the shelter of your constancy. Guard it within the globe of trust and detachment from all else but God, so that the evil whisperings of the ungodly may not extinguish its light. O My servants! My holy, My divinely ordained Revelation may be likened unto an ocean in whose depths are concealed innumerable pearls of great price, of surpassing luster. It is the duty of every seeker to bestir himself and strive to attain the shores of this ocean, so that he may, in proportion to the eagerness of his search and the efforts he hath exerted, partake of such benefits as have been pre-ordained in God's irrevocable and hidden Tablets. If no one be willing to direct his steps towards its shores, if every one should fail to arise and find Him, can such a failure be said to have robbed this ocean of its power or to have lessened, to any degree, its treasures? How vain, how contemptible, are the imaginations which your hearts have devised, and are still devising! O My servants! The one true God is My witness! This most great, this fathomless and surging Ocean is near, astonishingly near, unto you. Behold it is closer to you than your life-vein! Swift as the twinkling of an eye ye can, if ye but wish it, reach and partake of this imperishable favor, this God-given grace, this incorruptible gift, this most potent and unspeakably glorious bounty.

11.3   Whoso hath searched the depths of the oceans that lie hid within these exalted words, and fathomed their import, can be said to have discovered a glimmer of the unspeakable glory with which this mighty, this sublime, and most holy Revelation hath been endowed. From the excellence of so great a Revelation the honor with which its faithful followers must needs be invested can be well imagined. By the righteousness of the one true God! The very breath of these souls is in itself richer than all the treasures of the earth. Happy is the man that hath attained thereunto, and woe betide the heedless.

11.4 By the righteousness of God! These are the days in which God hath proved the hearts of the entire company of His Messengers and Prophets, and beyond them those that stand guard over His sacred and inviolable Sanctuary, the inmates of the celestial Pavilion and dwellers of the Tabernacle of Glory. How severe, therefore, the test to which they who join partners with God must needs be subjected!

11.5 Immerse yourselves in the ocean of My words, that ye may unravel its secrets, and discover all the pearls of wisdom that lie hid in its depths. Take heed that ye do not vacillate in your determination to embrace the truth of this Cause—a Cause through which the potentialities of the might of God have been revealed, and His sovereignty established. With faces beaming with joy, hasten ye unto Him. This is the changeless Faith of God, eternal in the past, eternal in the future. Let him that seeketh, attain it; and as to him that hath refused to seek it—verily, God is Self-Sufficient, above any need of His creatures.

11.6 Labor is needed, if we are to seek Him; ardor is needed, if we are to drink of the honey of reunion with Him; and if we taste of this cup, we shall cast away the world.

11.7 Blessed is the wayfarer who hath recognized the Desired One, and the seeker who hath heeded the Call of Him Who is the intended Aim of all mankind, and the learned one who hath believed in God, the Help in Peril, the Self-Subsisting.

11.8 The spirit that animateth the human heart is the knowledge of God...

11.9 Let it now be seen what thy search and endeavours will achieve.

FROM THE WRITINGS AND UTTERANCES OF 'ABDU'L-BAHÁ

11.10   Now, praise be to God, ye have shown will-power and have turned to the Sun of Truth. The plain of your hearts hath been illumined by the lights of the Lord of the Kingdom and ye have been led to the straight path, have marched along the road that leadeth to the Kingdom, have entered the Abha Paradise, and have secured a portion and share of the fruit of the Tree of Life.

      Blessed are ye and a goodly home awaiteth you. Upon you be greetings and praise.

11.11   O my Lord, they thirsted, Thou didst lift to their parched lips the waters of reunion. O Tender One, Bestowing One, Thou didst calm their pain with the balm of Thy bounty and grace, and didst heal their ailments with the sovereign medicine of Thy compassion. O Lord, make firm their feet on Thy straight path, make wide for them the needle's eye, and cause them, dressed in royal robes, to walk in glory for ever and ever.

11.12   O Lord, my God! Give me Thy grace to serve Thy loved ones, strengthen me in my servitude to Thee, illumine my brow with the light of adoration in Thy court of holiness, and of prayer to Thy Kingdom of grandeur. Help me to be selfless at the heavenly entrance of Thy gate, and aid me to be detached from all things within Thy holy precincts. Lord! Give me to drink from the chalice of selflessness; with its robe clothe me, and in its ocean immerse me. Make me as dust in the pathway of Thy loved ones, and grant that I may offer up my soul for the earth ennobled by the footsteps of Thy chosen ones in Thy path, O Lord of Glory in the Highest.

11.13   Every man trained through the teachings of God and illumined by the light of His guidance, who becomes a believer in God and His signs and is enkindled with the fire of the love of God, sacrifices the imperfections of nature for the sake of divine perfections. Consequently, every perfect person, every illumined, heavenly individual stands in the station of sacrifice. It is my hope that through the assistance and providence of God and through the bounties of the Kingdom of Abha you may be entirely severed from the imperfections of the world of nature, purified from selfish, human desires, receiving life from the Kingdom of Abha and attaining heavenly graces. May the divine light become manifest upon your faces, the fragrances of holiness refresh your nostrils and the breath of the Holy Spirit quicken you with eternal life.

FROM THE WRITINGS AND LETTERS WRITTEN BY, OR ON BEHALF OF, SHOGHI EFFENDI

11.14   Nor does the Bahá'í Revelation, claiming as it does to be the culmination of a prophetic cycle and the fulfillment of the promise of all ages, attempt, under any circumstances, to invalidate those first and everlasting principles that animate and underlie the religions that have preceded it. The God-given authority, vested in each one of them, it admits and establishes as its firmest and ultimate basis. It regards them in no other light except as different stages in the eternal history and constant evolution of one religion, Divine and indivisible, of which it itself forms but an integral part. It neither seeks to obscure their Divine origin, nor to dwarf the admitted magnitude of their colossal achievements. It can countenance no attempt that seeks to distort their features or to stultify the truths which they instill. Its teachings do not deviate a hairbreadth from the verities they enshrine, nor does the weight of its message detract one jot or one tittle from the influence they exert or the loyalty they inspire. Far from aiming at the overthrow of the spiritual foundation of the world's religious systems, its avowed, its unalterable purpose is to widen their basis, to restate their fundamentals, to reconcile their aims, to reinvigorate their life, to demonstrate their oneness, to restore the pristine purity of their teachings, to coordinate their functions and to assist in the realization of their highest aspirations. These divinely-revealed religions, as a close observer has graphically expressed it, "are doomed not to die, but to be reborn... 'Does not the child succumb in the youth and the youth in the man; yet neither child nor youth perishes?'"

FROM THE WRITINGS AND LETTERS WRITTEN BY, OR ON BEHALF OF, THE UNIVERSAL HOUSE OF JUSTICE

11.15 A Bahá'í recognizes that one aspect of his spiritual and intellectual growth is to foster the development of his conscience in the light of divine Revelation—a Revelation which, in addition to providing a wealth of spiritual and ethical principles, exhorts man "to free himself from idle fancy and imitation, discern with the eye of oneness His glorious handiwork, and look into all things with a searching eye". This process of development, therefore, involves a clear-sighted examination of the conditions of the world with both heart and mind. A Bahá'í will understand that an upright life is based upon observance of certain principles which stem from Divine Revelation and which he recognizes as essential for the well-being of both the individual and society. In order to uphold such principles, he knows that, in certain cases, the voluntary submission of the promptings of his own personal conscience to the decision of the majority is a conscientious requirement, as in wholeheartedly accepting the majority decision of an Assembly at the outcome of consultation.

11.16 In many of His utterances, 'Abdu'l-Bahá extols governments which uphold freedom of conscience for their citizens. As can be seen from the context, these statements refer to the freedom to follow the religion of one's choice. In the original of a passage to which you refer in your email of ..., He gives the following analysis of freedom.

There are three types of freedom. The first is divine freedom, which is one of the inherent attributes of the Creator for He is unconstrained in His will, and no one can force Him to change His decree in any matter whatsoever...."

The second is the political freedom of Europeans, which leaves the individual free to do whatsoever he desires as long as his action does not harm his neighbour. This is natural freedom, and its greatest expression is seen in the animal world. Observe these birds and notice with what freedom they live. However much man may try, he can never be as free as an animal, because the existence of order acts as an impediment to freedom."

The third freedom is that which is born of obedience to the laws and ordinances of the Almighty. This is the freedom of the human world, where man severs his affections from all things. When he does so, he becomes immune to all hardship and sorrow. Wealth or material power will not deflect him from moderation and fairness, neither will poverty or need inhibit him from showing forth happiness and tranquillity. The more the conscience of man develops, the more will his heart be free and his soul attain unto happiness. In the religion of God, there is freedom of thought because God, alone, controls the human conscience, but this freedom should not go beyond courtesy. In the religion of God, there is no freedom of action outside the law of God. Man may not transgress this law, even though no harm is inflicted on one's neighbour. This is because the purpose of Divine law is the education of all—others as well as oneself—and, in the sight of God, the harm done to one individual or to his neighbour is the same and is reprehensible in both cases. Hearts must possess the fear of God. Man should endeavour to avoid that which is abhorrent unto God. Therefore, the freedom that the laws of Europe offer to the individual does not exist in the law of God. Freedom of thought should not transgress the bounds of courtesy, and actions, likewise, should be governed by the fear of God and the desire to seek His good pleasure."

11.17 Let those seriously concerned about the state and fate of the world give due attention to the claims of Bahá'u'lláh. Let them realize that the storms battering at the foundations of society will not be stilled unless and until spiritual principles are actively engaged in the search for solutions to social problems.

CHAPTER 12:

CONCLUSION

FROM THE WRITINGS OF BAHÁ'U'LLÁH

12.1 Having created the world and all that liveth and moveth therein, He, through the direct operation of His unconstrained and sovereign Will, chose to confer upon man the unique distinction and capacity to know Him and to love Him—a capacity that must needs be regarded as the generating impulse and the primary purpose underlying the whole of creation.... Upon the inmost reality of each and every created thing He hath shed the light of one of His names, and made it a recipient of the glory of one of His attributes. Upon the reality of man, however, He hath focused the radiance of all of His names and attributes, and made it a mirror of His own Self. Alone of all created things man hath been singled out for so great a favor, so enduring a bounty.

12.2 O SON OF BEING! Busy not thyself with this world, for with fire We test the gold, and with gold We test Our servants.

12.3 Wouldst thou seek the grace of the Holy Spirit, enter into fellowship with the righteous...

12.4 The Prophets of God should be regarded as physicians whose task is to foster the well-being of the world and its peoples, that, through the spirit of oneness, they may heal the sickness of a divided humanity.

FROM THE WRITINGS AND UTTERANCES OF 'ABDU'L-BAHÁ

12.5 You must manifest complete love and affection toward all mankind. Do not exalt yourselves above others, but consider all as your equals, recognizing them as the servants of one God. Know that God is compassionate toward all; therefore, love all from the depths of your hearts, prefer all religionists before yourselves, be filled with love for every race, and be kind toward the people of all nationalities. Never speak disparagingly of others, but praise without distinction. Pollute not your tongues by speaking evil of another.

12.6 The people must be so attracted to you that they will exclaim, 'What happiness exists among you!' and will see in your faces the lights of the Kingdom; then in wonderment they will turn to you and seek the cause of your happiness. You must give the message through action and deed, not alone by word. Word must be conjoined with deed. You must love your friend better than yourself; yes, be willing to sacrifice yourself. The Cause of Bahá'u'lláh has not yet appeared in this country. I desire that you be ready to sacrifice everything for each other, even life itself; then I will know that the Cause of Bahá'u'lláh has been established.

12.7 God has created His servants in order that they may love and associate with each other. He has revealed the glorious splendor of His sun of love in the world of humanity. The cause of the creation of the phenomenal world is love. All the Prophets have promulgated the law of love. Man has opposed the will of God and acted in opposition to the plan of God. Therefore, from the beginning of history to the present time the world of humanity has had no lasting rest; warfare and strife have continuously prevailed, and hearts have manifested hatred toward each other. The cause of bloodshed and battle, strife and hatred throughout the past has been either religious, racial, patriotic or political prejudice. Therefore, the world of humanity has ever been in torment. These prejudices are more pronounced in the Orient, where freedom is restricted. In the nineteenth century the nations of the East were restless and in a state of inner commotion. The darkness of imitations and forms had enveloped religious belief. The people of religions were in constant warfare, filled with enmity, hatred and bitterness. In the midst of these conditions Bahá'u'lláh appeared. He proclaimed the oneness of the world of humanity and announced that all are the servants of God. He taught that all the religions are beneath the shadow and protection of the Almighty, that God is compassionate and loving to all, that the revelations of all the Prophets of the past have been in perfect unity and agreement, that the heavenly Books have confirmed each other; therefore, why should contention and strife exist among the people?

12.8 Furthermore, those souls who have followed Bahá'u'lláh and attained this condition of fellowship and affiliation are Muslims, Jews, Christians, Zoroastrians, Buddhists, Nestorians, Sunnites, Shiites and others. No discord exists among them. This is a proof of the possibility of unification among the religionists of the world through practical means. Imitations and prejudices which have held men apart have been discarded, and the reality of religion envelops them in a perfect unity. When reality envelops the soul of man, love is possible. The divine purpose in religion is pure love and agreement. The Prophets of God manifested complete love for all. Each One announced the glad tidings of His successor, and each subsequent One confirmed the teachings and prophecies of the Prophet Who preceded Him. There was no disagreement or variance in the reality of Their teaching and mission. Discord has arisen among Their followers, who have lost sight of reality and hold fast to imitations. If imitations be done away with and the radiant shining reality dawn in the souls of men, love and unity must prevail. In this way humanity will be rescued from the strife and wars which have prevailed for thousands of years; dissensions will pass away and the illumination of unity dawn. Consider how all the Prophets of God were persecuted and what hardships They experienced. Jesus Christ endured affliction and accepted martyrdom upon the cross in order to summon mankind to unity and love. What sacrifice could be greater? He brought the religion of love and fellowship into the world. Shall we make use of it to create discord, violence and hatred among mankind?

12.9 God, the Almighty, has created all mankind from the dust of earth. He has fashioned them all from the same elements; they are descended from the same race and live upon the same globe. He has created them to dwell beneath the one heaven. As members of the human family and His children He has endowed them with equal susceptibilities. He maintains, protects and is kind to all. He has made no distinction in mercies and graces among His children. With impartial love and wisdom He has sent forth His Prophets and divine teachings. His teachings are the means of establishing union and fellowship among mankind and awakening love and kindness in human hearts. He proclaims the oneness of the kingdom of humanity. He rebukes those things which create differences and destroy harmony; He commends and praises every means that will conduce to the solidarity of the human race. He encourages man in every step of advancement which leads to ultimate union. The Prophets of God have been inspired with the message of love and unity. The Books of God have been revealed for the upbuilding of fellowship and union. The Prophets of God have been the servants of reality; Their teachings constitute the science of reality. Reality is one; it does not admit plurality. We conclude, therefore, that the foundation of the religions of God is one foundation. Notwithstanding this, certain forms and imitations have been persistently adhered to which have nothing to do with the foundation of the teachings of the Prophets of God. As these imitations are various and different, contention and strife prevail among the people of religious beliefs, and the foundation of the religion of God has become obscured. Like beasts of prey, men are warring and killing each other, destroying cities and homes, devastating countries and kingdoms.

12.10 The greatest attainment in the world of humanity is nearness to God. Every lasting glory, honor, grace and beauty which comes to man comes through nearness to God. All the Prophets and apostles longed and prayed for nearness to the Creator. How many nights they passed in sleepless yearning for this station; how many days they devoted to supplication for this attainment, seeking ever to draw nigh unto Him! But nearness to God is not an easy accomplishment. During the time Jesus Christ was upon the earth mankind sought nearness to God, but in that day no one attained it save a very few—His disciples. Those blessed souls were confirmed with divine nearness through the love of God. Divine nearness is dependent upon attainment to the knowledge of God, upon severance from all else save God. It is contingent upon self-sacrifice and to be found only through forfeiting wealth and worldly possessions. It is made possible through the baptism of water and fire revealed in the Gospels. Water symbolizes the water of life, which is knowledge, and fire is the fire of the love of God; therefore, man must be baptized with the water of life, the Holy Spirit and the fire of the love of the Kingdom. Until he attains these three degrees, nearness to God is not possible. This is the process by which the

Bahá'ís of Persia have attained it. They gave their lives for this station, sacrificed honor, comfort and possessions, hastened with the utmost joy to the place of martyrdom; their blood was spilled, their bodies were tortured and destroyed, their homes pillaged, their children carried into captivity. They endured all these conditions joyfully and willingly. Through such sacrifice nearness to God is made possible. And be it known that this nearness is not dependent upon time or place. Nearness to God is dependent upon purity of the heart and exhilaration of the spirit through the glad tidings of the Kingdom. Consider how a pure, well-polished mirror fully reflects the effulgence of the sun, no matter how distant the sun may be. As soon as the mirror is cleaned and purified, the sun will manifest itself. The more pure and sanctified the heart of man becomes, the nearer it draws to God, and the light of the Sun of Reality is revealed within it. This light sets hearts aglow with the fire of the love of God, opens in them the doors of knowledge and unseals the divine mysteries so that spiritual discoveries are made possible. All the Prophets have drawn near to God through severance. We must emulate those Holy Souls and renounce our own wishes and desires. We must purify ourselves from the mire and soil of earthly contact until our hearts become as mirrors in clearness and the light of the most great guidance reveals itself in them.

12.11 As to you: Your efforts must be lofty. Exert yourselves with heart and soul so that, perchance, through your efforts the light of universal peace may shine and this darkness of estrangement and enmity may be dispelled from amongst men, that all men may become as one family and consort together in love and kindness, that the East may assist the West and the West give help to the East, for all are the inhabitants of one planet, the people of one original native land and the flocks of one Shepherd.

Consider how the Prophets Who have been sent, the great souls who have appeared and the sages who have arisen in the world have exhorted mankind to unity and love. This has been the essence of their mission and teaching. This has been the goal of their guidance and message. The Prophets, saints, seers and philosophers have sacrificed their lives in order to establish these principles and teachings amongst men. Consider the heedlessness of the world, for notwithstanding the efforts and sufferings of the Prophets of God, the nations and peoples are still engaged in hostility and fighting. Notwithstanding the heavenly commandments to love one another, they are still shedding each other's blood. How heedless and ignorant are the people of the world! How gross the darkness which envelops them! Although they are the children of a compassionate God, they continue to live and act in opposition to His will and good pleasure. God is loving and kind to all men, and yet they show the utmost enmity and hatred toward each other. God is the Giver of life to them, and yet they constantly seek to destroy life. God blesses and protects their homes; they rage, sack and destroy each other's homes. Consider their ignorance and heedlessness!

Your duty is of another kind, for you are informed of the mysteries of God. Your eyes are illumined; your ears are quickened with hearing. You must, therefore, look toward each other and then toward mankind with the utmost love and kindness. You have no excuse to bring before God if you fail to live according to His command, for you are informed of that which constitutes the good pleasure of God. You have heard His commandments and precepts. You must, therefore, be kind to all men; you must even treat your enemies as your friends. You must consider your evil-wishers as your well-wishers. Those who are not agreeable toward you must be regarded as those who are congenial and pleasant so that, perchance, this darkness of disagreement and conflict may disappear from amongst men and the light of the divine may shine forth, so that the Orient may be illumined and the Occident filled with fragrance, nay, so that the East and West may embrace each other in love and deal with one another in sympathy and affection. Until man reaches this high station, the world of humanity shall not find rest, and eternal felicity shall not be attained. But if man lives up to these divine commandments, this world of earth shall be transformed into the world of heaven, and this material sphere shall be converted into a paradise of glory. It is my hope that you may become successful in this high calling so that like brilliant lamps you may cast light upon the world of humanity and quicken and stir the body of existence like unto a spirit of life. This is eternal glory. This is everlasting felicity. This is immortal life. This is heavenly attainment. This is being created in the image and likeness of God. And unto this I call you, praying to God to strengthen and bless you.

FROM THE WRITINGS AND LETTERS WRITTEN BY, OR ON BEHALF OF, SHOGHI EFFENDI

12.12 Dearly beloved friends: Who, contemplating the helplessness, the fears and miseries of humanity in this day, can any longer question the necessity for a fresh revelation of the quickening power of God's redemptive love and guidance? Who, witnessing on one hand the stupendous advance achieved in the realm of human knowledge, of power, of skill and inventiveness, and viewing on the other the unprecedented character of the sufferings that afflict, and the dangers that beset, present-day society, can be so blind as to doubt that the hour has at last struck for the advent of a new Revelation, for a re-statement of the Divine Purpose, and for the consequent revival of those spiritual forces that have, at fixed intervals, rehabilitated the fortunes of human society? Does not the very operation of the world-unifying forces that are at work in this age necessitate that He Who is the Bearer of the Message of God in this day should not only reaffirm that self-same exalted standard of individual conduct inculcated by the Prophets gone before Him, but embody in His appeal, to all governments and peoples, the essentials of that social code, that Divine Economy, which must guide humanity's concerted efforts in establishing that all-embracing federation which is to signalize the advent of the Kingdom of God on this earth?

FROM THE WRITINGS AND LETTERS WRITTEN BY, OR ON BEHALF OF, THE UNIVERSAL HOUSE OF JUSTICE

12.13 A Bahá'í's duty to pursue an unfettered search after truth should lead him to understand the Teachings as an organic, logically coherent whole, should cause him to examine his own ideas and motives, and should enable him to see that adherence to the Covenant, to which he is a party, is not blind imitation but conscious choice, freely made and freely followed.

APPENDIX:

SOURCES AND BIBLIOGRAPHY

SOURCES FOR MANY PATHS TO THE BAHÁ'Í FAITH

Chapter 1
1.1   Bahá'u'lláh, The Seven Valleys, p. 4
1.2   Bahá'u'lláh, The Kitáb-i-Iqan, p. 194
1.3   Bahá'u'lláh, Gleanings from the Writings of Bahá'u'lláh, p. 9
1.4   Bahá'u'lláh, Gleanings from the Writings of Bahá'u'lláh, p. 320
1.5   'Abdu'l-Bahá, Selections from the Writings of 'Abdu'l-Bahá, p. 41
1.6   'Abdu'l-Bahá, Selections from the Writings of 'Abdu'l-Bahá, p. 316
1.7   'Abdu'l-Bahá, Selections from the Writings of 'Abdu'l-Bahá, p. 168
1.8   'Abdu'l-Bahá, Selections from the Writings of 'Abdu'l-Bahá, p. 190
1.9   'Abdu'l-Bahá, Selections from the Writings of 'Abdu'l-Bahá, p. 14
1.10 'Abdu'l-Bahá, Some Answered Questions, p. 239
1.11 Shoghi Effendi, The Promised Day is Come, p. 108
1.12 From a letter written on behalf of Shoghi Effendi to an individual believer, March 3, 1955Lights of Guidance, p. 209

Chapter 2
2.1   Bahá'u'lláh, Gleanings from the Writings of Bahá'u'lláh, p. 10
2.2   Bahá'u'lláh, The Proclamation of Bahá'u'lláh
2.3   Baha'u'llah, Epistle to the Son of the Wolf, p. 24
2.4   Baha'u'llah, The Kitab-i-Aqdas, p. 73
2.5   Baha'u'llah, Epistle to the Son of the Wolf, p. 11
2.6   Baha'u'llah, The Summons of the Lord of Hosts, p. 4
2.7   'Abdu'l-Bahá, Selections from the Writings of 'Abdu'l-Bahá, p. 100
2.8   'Abdu'l-Bahá, Selections from the Writings of 'Abdu'l-Bahá, p. 252
2.9   'Abdu'l-Bahá, The Promulgation of Universal Peace, p. 105
2.10 'Abdu'l-Bahá, The Promulgation of Universal Peace, p. 313
2.11 'Abdu'l-Bahá, The Promulgation of Universal Peace, p. 28
2.12 Shoghi Effendi, Summary Statement - 1947, Special UN Committee on Palestine
2.13 Shoghi Effendi, God Passes By, p. 281
2.14 The Universal House of Justice, 1985 Oct, The Promise of World Peace, p. 1
2.15 The Universal House of Justice, 1985 Oct, The Promise of World Peace, p. 1

Chapter 3
3.1   Bahá'u'lláh, Gleanings from the Writings of Bahá'u'lláh, p. 10
3.2   Bahá'u'lláh, Gleanings from the Writings of Bahá'u'lláh, p. 17
3.3   Bahá'u'lláh, Gleanings from the Writings of Bahá'u'lláh, p. 17
3.4   Bahá'u'lláh, Gleanings from the Writings of Bahá'u'lláh, p. 200
3.5   Bahá'u'lláh, Gleanings from the Writings of Bahá'u'lláh, p. 142
3.6   Bahá'u'lláh, Gleanings from the Writings of Bahá'u'lláh, p. 264
3.7   Bahá'u'lláh, The Seven Valleys, p. 4
3.8   Bahá'u'lláh, The Seven Valleys, p. 40
3.9   Bahá'u'lláh, The Seven Valleys, p. 7
3.10 Bahá'u'lláh, The Seven Valleys, p. 24
3.11 'Abdu'l-Bahá, The Promulgation of Universal Peace, p. 295
3.12 'Abdu'l-Bahá, The Promulgation of Universal Peace, p. 295
3.13 'Abdu'l-Bahá, The Promulgation of Universal Peace, p. 416
3.14 'Abdu'l-Bahá, The Promulgation of Universal Peace, p. 62
3.15 'Abdu'l-Bahá, The Promulgation of Universal Peace, p. 463
3.16 'Abdu'l-Bahá, Paris Talks, p. 135
3.17 Shoghi Effendi, The Promised Day is Come, p. v
3.18 From a Letter Written on Behalf of Shoghi Effendi, 22 April 1954 to an individual believerCompilation on Scholarship, p. 16

168 ❓ Many Paths to the Bahá'í Faith: QUOTATIONS

3.19   From a letter written on behalf of Shoghi Effendi to an individual believer, December 10, 1947. Lights of Guidance, p. 113
3.20   From a letter written on behalf of Shoghi Effendi to an individual believer, October 3, 1943. Lights of Guidance, p. 209
3.21   The Universal House of Justice, Messages 1963 to 1986, p. 389
3.22   The Universal House of Justice, Messages 1963 to 1986, p. 390
3.23   From a letter written on behalf of the Universal House of Justice to the National Spiritual Assembly of Bolivia, October 16, 1979. Lights of Guidance, p. 477
3.24   Bahá'í International Community, 1995 Jan 10, Promoting Religious Tolerance
3.25   Bahá'í International Community, 1988 Feb 17, Eliminating Religious Intolerance

Chapter 4
4.1   Bahá'u'lláh, Gleanings from the Writings of Bahá'u'lláh, p. 18
4.2   Bahá'u'lláh, Gleanings from the Writings of Bahá'u'lláh, p. 12
4.3   Bahá'u'lláh, Gleanings from the Writings of Bahá'u'lláh, p. 56
4.4   Bahá'u'lláh, Gleanings from the Writings of Bahá'u'lláh, p. 75
4.5   Bahá'u'lláh, Gleanings from the Writings of Bahá'u'lláh, p. 17
4.6   'Abdu'l-Bahá, The Promulgation of Universal Peace, p. 127
4.7   'Abdu'l-Bahá, The Promulgation of Universal Peace, p. 340
4.8   'Abdu'l-Bahá, The Promulgation of Universal Peace, p. 368
4.9   'Abdu'l-Bahá, The Promulgation of Universal Peace, p. 406
4.10   'Abdu'l-Bahá, The Promulgation of Universal Peace, p. 366
4.11   'Abdu'l-Bahá, The Promulgation of Universal Peace, p. 407
4.12   'Abdu'l-Bahá, The Promulgation of Universal Peace, p. 291
4.13   'Abdu'l-Bahá, The Promulgation of Universal Peace, p. 363
4.14   'Abdu'l-Bahá, Paris Talks, p. 119
4.15   'Abdu'l-Bahá: Daily Lessons Received at 'Akká p. 45, 1979 ed. Lights of Guidance, p. 499
4.16   'Abdu'l-Bahá: Secret of Divine Civilization, p. 77
4.17   According to information received by the National Spiritual Assembly of the United States several years ago this Tablet was revealed by the Master in the year 1897 to a Jewish Community in the Orient: Bahá'í News. No. 250. December 1951. p. 5. Lights of Guidance, p. 499
4.18   From a letter written on behalf of Shoghi Effendi to an individual believer, July 11, 1942. Lights of Guidance, p. 472
4.19   From a letter written behalf of Shoghi Effendi to an individual believer, September 22, 1937. Lights of Guidance, p. 534
4.20   From a letter written on behalf of the Guardian to an individual believer, April 21, 1939. Lights of Guidance, p. 498
4.21   From letter of Shoghi Effendi to the chairman of the United Nations Special Committee on Palestine, July 14, 1947: Bahá'í News. No. 199, September 1947. p. 3. Lights of Guidance, p. 498
4.22   From a letter written on behalf of Shoghi Effendi to an individual believer, March 15, 1948. Lights of Guidance, p. 535
4.23   The Universal House of Justice, Messages 1963 to 1986, p. 396
4.24   From a letter written on behalf of the Universal House of Justice to an individual believer, March 13, 1986. Lights of Guidance, p. 500

Chapter 5
5.1   Bahá'u'lláh, Tablets of Bahá'u'lláh, p. 12
5.2   Bahá'u'lláh, Gleanings from the Writings of Bahá'u'lláh, p. 85
5.3   Bahá'u'lláh, Gleanings from the Writings of Bahá'u'lláh, p. 83
5.4   Bahá'u'lláh, The Kitáb-i-Iqan, p. 17
5.5   Bahá'u'lláh, Gleanings from the Writings of Bahá'u'lláh, p. 20
5.6   Bahá'u'lláh, Gleanings from the Writings of Bahá'u'lláh, p. 20
5.7   Bahá'u'lláh, Gleanings from the Writings of Bahá'u'lláh, p. 86
5.8   'Abdu'l-Bahá, Selections from the Writings of 'Abdu'l-Bahá, p. 12

5.9	'Abdu'l-Bahá, Selections from the Writings of 'Abdu'l-Bahá, p. 175
5.10	'Abdu'l-Bahá, Selections from the Writings of 'Abdu'l-Bahá, p. 58
5.11	'Abdu'l-Bahá, Selections from the Writings of 'Abdu'l-Bahá, p. 303
5.12	'Abdu'l-Bahá, Selections from the Writings of 'Abdu'l-Bahá, p. 44
5.13	Abdu'l-Baha, Tablets of the Divine Plan, p. 56
5.14	'Abdu'l-Bahá, Selections from the Writings of 'Abdu'l-Bahá, p. 59
5.15	'Abdu'l-Bahá, Selections from the Writings of 'Abdu'l-Bahá, p. 167
5.16	'Abdu'l-Bahá, Selections from the Writings of 'Abdu'l-Bahá, p. 198
5.17	'Abdu'l-Bahá, Some Answered Questions, p. 36
5.18	'Abdu'l-Bahá, Some Answered Questions, p. 89
5.19	'Abdu'l-Bahá, Some Answered Questions, p. 93
5.20	'Abdu'l-Bahá, The Promulgation of Universal Peace, p. 5
5.21	'Abdu'l-Bahá, The Promulgation of Universal Peace, p. 291
5.22	'Abdu'l-Bahá, 'Abdu'l-Bahá in London, p. 92
5.23	'Abdu'l-Bahá, The Promulgation of Universal Peace, p. 288
5.24	From a letter written on behalf of the Guardian to an individual believer, March 12, 1949: Bahá'í News, No.251, p. 2, January 1952. Lights of Guidance, p. 68
5.25	From a letter written on behalf of the Guardian to two believers, August 17, 1941. Lights of Guidance, p. 491
5.26	From a letter written to an individual believer on behalf of the Guardian, August 14, 1934. Lights of Guidance, p. 492
5.27	The Universal House of Justice, 1998 Dec 16, Traditional practices in Africa

Chapter 6

6.1	Bahá'u'lláh, The Kitáb-i-Iqan, p. 153
6.2	Bahá'u'lláh, The Kitáb-i-Iqan, p. 20
6.3	Bahá'u'lláh, The Kitáb-i-Iqan, p. 161
6.4	Bahá'u'lláh, The Kitáb-i-Iqan, p. 135
6.5	Bahá'u'lláh, Gleanings from the Writings of Bahá'u'lláh, p. 83
6.6	Bahá'u'lláh, The Kitáb-i-Iqan, p. 15
6.7	Bahá'u'lláh, The Kitáb-i-Iqan, p. 167
6.8	Bahá'u'lláh, The Kitáb-i-Iqan, p. 168
6.9	Bahá'u'lláh, The Kitáb-i-Iqan, p. 24
6.10	Bahá'u'lláh, The Kitáb-i-Iqan, p. 26
6.11	'Abdu'l-Bahá, The Promulgation of Universal Peace, p. 117
6.12	'Abdu'l-Bahá, Paris Talks, p. 48
6.13	'Abdu'l-Bahá, The Promulgation of Universal Peace, p. 367
6.14	'Abdu'l-Bahá, The Promulgation of Universal Peace, p. 346
6.15	'Abdu'l-Bahá, The Promulgation of Universal Peace, p. 409
6.16	'Abdu'l-Bahá, The Promulgation of Universal Peace, p. 366
6.17	From a letter written on behalf of the Guardian by his secretary to an individual believer, November 19, 1945: Bahá'í News, No. 210, p. 3, August 1948. Lights of Guidance, p. 494
6.18	From a letter written on behalf of Shoghi Effendi to an individual believer, April 27, 1936. Lights of Guidance, p. 495
6.19	From a letter written on behalf of the Guardian to an individual believer, August 22, 1939:Bahá'í News, No. 134,pp. 2-3, March 1940. Lights of Guidance, p. 496
6.20	From a letter written on behalf of the Guardian to an individual believer, March 19, 1938. Lights of Guidance, p. 497
6.21	From a letter written on behalf of the Guardian to an individual believer, January 29, 1939. Lights of Guidance, p. 497
6.22	From a letter written on behalf of Shoghi Effendi to an individual believer, July 30, 1941. Lights of Guidance, p. 496
6.23	The Universal House of Justice, Messages 1963 to 1986, p. 396
6.24	The Universal House of Justice, Messages 1963 to 1986, p. 460
6.25	The Universal House of Justice, Messages 1963 to 1986, p. 460
6.26	Qu'ran, 2:87
6.27	The Qur'an E.H. Palmer tr, Sura 2 - The Heifer

170 ❓ Many Paths to the Bahá'í Faith: QUOTATIONS

Chapter 7
7.1   Bahá'u'lláh, The Hidden Words, Persian #27
7.2   Bahá'u'lláh, Gleanings from the Writings of Bahá'u'lláh, p. 61
7.3   Bahá'u'lláh, Gleanings from the Writings of Bahá'u'lláh, p. 155
7.4   Bahá'u'lláh, The Hidden Words, Persian #29
7.5   Bahá'u'lláh, Gleanings from the Writings of Bahá'u'lláh, p. 171
7.6   Bahá'u'lláh, Gleanings from the Writings of Bahá'u'lláh, p. 94
7.7   Bahá'u'lláh, Gleanings from the Writings of Bahá'u'lláh, p. 27
7.8   Bahá'u'lláh, Gleanings from the Writings of Bahá'u'lláh, p. 149
7.9   Bahá'u'lláh, Prayers and Meditations by Bahá'u'lláh, p. 42
7.10 'Abdu'l-Bahá, Selections from the Writings of 'Abdu'l-Bahá, p. 56
7.11 'Abdu'l-Bahá, Selections from the Writings of 'Abdu'l-Bahá, p. 27
7.12 'Abdu'l-Bahá, Selections from the Writings of 'Abdu'l-Bahá, p. 183
7.13 'Abdu'l-Bahá, Selections from the Writings of 'Abdu'l-Bahá, p. 183
7.14 'Abdu'l-Bahá, Selections from the Writings of 'Abdu'l-Bahá, p. 156
7.15 'Abdu'l-Bahá, Selections from the Writings of 'Abdu'l-Bahá, p. 198
7.16 'Abdu'l-Bahá, Some Answered Questions, p. 283
7.17 'Abdu'l-Bahá, Paris Talks, p. 37
7.18 'Abdu'l-Bahá, The Promulgation of Universal Peace, p. 346
7.19 'Abdu'l-Bahá, The Promulgation of Universal Peace, p. 170
7.20 'Abdu'l-Bahá, Paris Talks, p. 138
7.21 'Abdu'l-Bahá, Paris Talks, p. 146
7.22 Shoghi Effendi, Dawn of a New Day, p. 12
7.23 Shoghi Effendi, Dawn of a New Day, p. 198
7.24 Shoghi Effendi, Dawn of a New Day, p. 198
7.25 Shoghi Effendi, Dawn of a New Day, p. 201
7.26 From a letter written on behalf of Shoghi Effendi to an individual believer, April 22, 1954. Lights of Guidance, p. 538
7.27 The Universal House of Justice, Ridvan 153, 1996 - Bangladesh, India, Nepal...
7.28 The Universal House of Justice, 1996 Aug 06,, The Compilation of Compilations vol. I, p. 20
7.29 From a letter written on behalf of the Universal House of Justice to the National Spiritual Assembly of Bolivia, October 16, 1979. Lights of Guidance, p. 477
7.30 From a letter dated September 1, 1977 written on behalf of the Universal House of Justice to an individual believer The Universal House of Justice, 1981 Jan 01, Other Holy Scriptures
7.31 Bhagavad Gita

Chapter 8
8.1   Bahá'u'lláh, The Hidden Words, Arabic #52
8.2   Bahá'u'lláh, Gleanings from the Writings of Bahá'u'lláh, p. 255
8.3   Bahá'u'lláh, The Hidden Words, Persian #51
8.4   Bahá'u'lláh, Tablets of Bahá'u'lláh, p. 14
8.5   Bahá'u'lláh, Epistle to the Son of the Wolf, p. 49
8.6   Bahá'u'lláh, Gleanings from the Writings of Bahá'u'lláh, p. 46
8.7   Bahá'u'lláh, The Hidden Words, Persian #14
8.8   Bahá'u'lláh, The Hidden Words, Arabic #56
8.9   Bahá'u'lláh, The Hidden Words, Persian #40
8.10 Bahá'u'lláh, Prayers and Meditations by Bahá'u'lláh, p. 132
8.11 Bahá'u'lláh, Gleanings from the Writings of Bahá'u'lláh, p. 337
8.12 'Abdu'l-Bahá, Selections from the Writings of 'Abdu'l-Bahá, p. 206
8.13 'Abdu'l-Bahá, Selections from the Writings of 'Abdu'l-Bahá, p. 152
8.14 'Abdu'l-Bahá, Selections from the Writings of 'Abdu'l-Bahá, p. 76
8.15 'Abdu'l-Bahá, Some Answered Questions, p. 165
8.16 'Abdu'l-Bahá, 'Abdu'l-Bahá in London, p. 120
8.17 'Abdu'l-Bahá, Bahá'í World Faith - 'Abdu'l-Bahá Section, p. 378
8.18 'Abdu'l-Bahá, Paris Talks, p. 110

Appendix: Sources and Bibliography   171

8.19	'Abdu'l-Bahá, The Promulgation of Universal Peace, p. 244
8.20	'Abdu'l-Bahá, The Promulgation of Universal Peace, p. 304
8.21	'Abdu'l-Bahá, The Promulgation of Universal Peace, p. 304
8.22	'Abdu'l-Bahá, The Promulgation of Universal Peace, p. 301
8.23	'Abdu'l-Bahá, The Promulgation of Universal Peace, p. 355
8.24	'Abdu'l-Bahá, 'Abdu'l-Bahá in London, p. 93
8.25	'Abdu'l-Bahá, The Promulgation of Universal Peace, p. 346
8.26	'Abdu'l-Bahá, 'Abdu'l-Bahá in London, p. 63
8.27	Shoghi Effendi, God Passes By, p. 95
8.28	From a letter written on behalf of the Guardian to the National Spiritual Assembly of Australia and New Zealand, December 26, 1941: Letter from the Guardian to Australia and New Zealand, 1923-1957, p. 41. Lights of Guidance, p. 500
8.29	The Universal House of Justice, Ridvan 153, 1996 - Cambodia, Hong Kong, Macau, Malaysia...
8.30	The Universal House of Justice, Ridvan 153, 1996 - Cambodia, Hong Kong, Macau, Malaysia...
8.31	Digha-nikaya, IV.26
8.32	DN, Mahaparinibbana-Suttana 3:76
8.33	Tevigga Sutra, 'Buddhist Bible', Dwight Goddard translations
8.34	Awakening of Faith, 'Buddhist Bible', Dwight Goddard translations

Chapter 9

9.1	Bahá'u'lláh, Prayers and Meditations, p. 272
9.2	Bahá'u'lláh, Epistle to the Son of the Wolf, p. 44
9.3	Bahá'u'lláh, The Hidden Words, Arabic #68
9.4	Bahá'u'lláh, Gleanings from the Writings of Bahá'u'lláh, p. 32
9.5	Bahá'u'lláh, Gems of Divine Mysteries, p. 60
9.6	Bahá'u'lláh, Gleanings from the Writings of Bahá'u'lláh, p. 7
9.7	Bahá'u'lláh, Gleanings from the Writings of Bahá'u'lláh, p. 303
9.8	Bahá'u'lláh, The Hidden Words, Persian #36
9.9	Bahá'u'lláh, The Hidden Words, Persian #43
9.10	Bahá'u'lláh, The Hidden Words, Persian #2
9.11	Bahá'u'lláh, quoted by the Bahá'í International Community in The Bahá'í Statement on Nature
9.12	Bahá'u'lláh, Gleanings from the Writings of Bahá'u'lláh, p. 215
9.13	Abdu'l-Bahá, in Tablets of the Divine Plan, pp. 31-32
9.14	'Abdu'l-Bahá, Selections from the Writings of 'Abdu'l-Bahá, p. 233
9.15	'Abdu'l-Bahá, Selections from the Writings of 'Abdu'l-Bahá, p. 256
9.16	'Abdu'l-Bahá, Selections from the Writings of 'Abdu'l-Bahá, p. 241
9.17	'Abdu'l-Bahá, Selections from the Writings of 'Abdu'l-Bahá, p. 31
9.18	'Abdu'l-Bahá, 'Abdu'l-Bahá in London, p. 19
9.19	'Abdu'l-Bahá, The Promulgation of Universal Peace, p. 99
9.20	Shoghi Effendi, The Advent of Divine Justice, p. 45
9.21	Shoghi Effendi, Citadel of Faith, p. 16
9.22	From a letter written on behalf of Shoghi Effendi to an individual believer, March 19, 1945. Lights of Guidance, p. 542
9.23	From a letter written on behalf of Shoghi Effendi to an individual believer, August 2, 1955. Lights of Guidance, p. 577
9.24	From a letter written on behalf of Shoghi Effendi to the Comite Nacional de Ensenanza Bahá'í para los Indigenas de Sur America, September 21, 1951. Lights of Guidance, p. 523
9.25	From a letter written on behalf of Shoghi Effendi to the National Spiritual Assembly of Meso-America and the Antilles, July 11, 1951: A special Measure of Love. p. 5. Lights of Guidance, p. 523
9.26	From a letter written on behalf of Shoghi Effendi to an individual believer, December 21, 1947. Lights of Guidance, p. 530
9.27	The Universal House of Justice, Messages 1963 to 1986, p. 329
9.28	The Universal House of Justice, Messages 1963 to 1986, p. 329

9.29	The Universal House of Justice, Ridvan 153, 1996 - Australia, the Cook Islands...
9.30	The Universal House of Justice, Ridvan 153, 1996 - North America, p. 1
9.31	Bahá'í International Community, 1988 Aug 01, Rights of Indigenous Populations

Chapter 10

10.1	Bahá'u'lláh, Gleanings from the Writings of Bahá'u'lláh p. 73
10.2	Bahá'u'lláh, Gleanings from the Writings of Bahá'u'lláh, p. 46
10.3	Bahá'u'lláh, Gleanings from the Writings of Bahá'u'lláh, p. 48
10.4	Bahá'u'lláh, Gleanings from the Writings of Bahá'u'lláh, p. 147
10.5	Bahá'u'lláh, Tablets of Bahá'u'lláh, p. 141
10.6	Bahá'u'lláh, Tablets of Bahá'u'lláh, p. 145
10.7	Bahá'u'lláh, Tablets of Bahá'u'lláh, p. 146
10.8	Bahá'u'lláh, Tablets of Bahá'u'lláh, p. 168
10.9	Bahá'u'lláh, Tablets of Bahá'u'lláh, p. 168
10.10	Bahá'u'lláh, Gleanings from the Writings of Bahá'u'lláh, p. 342
10.11	Bahá'u'lláh, The Kitáb-i-Iqan, p. 164
10.12	Bahá'u'lláh, Gleanings from the Writings of Bahá'u'lláh, p. 335
10.13	Bahá'u'lláh, Tablets of Bahá'u'lláh, p. 25
10.14	'Abdu'l-Bahá, Selections from the Writings of 'Abdu'l-Bahá, p. 58
10.15	'Abdu'l-Bahá, Selections from the Writings of 'Abdu'l-Bahá, p. 288
10.16	'Abdu'l-Bahá, Selections from the Writings of 'Abdu'l-Bahá pg. 6
10.17	'Abdu'l-Bahá, Selections from the Writings of 'Abdu'l-Bahá, p. 302
10.18	'Abdu'l-Bahá, Selections from the Writings of 'Abdu'l-Bahá, p. 303
10.19	'Abdu'l-Bahá, Selections from the Writings of 'Abdu'l-Bahá, p. 53
10.20	'Abdu'l-Bahá, Some Answered Questions, p. 37
10.21	'Abdu'l-Bahá, Some Answered Questions, p. 101
10.22	'Abdu'l-Bahá, The Promulgation of Universal Peace, p. 21
10.23	'Abdu'l-Bahá, The Promulgation of Universal Peace, p. 325
10.24	'Abdu'l-Bahá, The Promulgation of Universal Peace, p. 40
10.25	'Abdu'l-Bahá, The Promulgation of Universal Peace, p. 292
10.26	'Abdu'l-Bahá, The Promulgation of Universal Peace, p. 454
10.27	'Abdu'l-Bahá, Paris Talks, p. 122
10.28	'Abdu'l-Bahá, 'Abdu'l-Bahá in London, p. 19
10.29	'Abdu'l-Bahá, 'Abdu'l-Bahá in London, p. 28
10.30	'Abdu'l-Bahá, 'Abdu'l-Bahá in London, p. 79
10.31	'Abdu'l-Bahá, 'Abdu'l-Bahá in London, p. 28
10.32	Abdu'l-Baha, The Promulgation of Universal Peace, p. 174
10.33	From a letter written on behalf of Shoghi Effendi to an individual believer, March 19, 1945. Lights of Guidance, p. 542
10.34	From a letter written on behalf of Shoghi Effendi to an individual believer, February 26, 1933: Bahá'í News, No. 80, p. 5 January 1934. Lights of Guidance, p. 474
10.35	From a letter written on behalf of the Guardian to an individual believer, December 8, 1935. Lights of Guidance, p. 134
10.36	Letter written on behalf of the Guardian to an individual believer, October 18, 1932. Lights of Guidance, p. 212
10.37	Letter from the Guardian to an individual believer, December 8, 1935; Bahá'í Youth, p. 10. Lights of Guidance, p. 543
10.38	The Universal House of Justice, Messages 1963 to 1986, p. 27
10.39	The Universal House of Justice, Messages 1963 to 1986, p. 339
10.40	The Universal House of Justice, Messages 1963 to 1986, p. 390
10.41	The Universal House of Justice, Messages 1963 to 1986, p. 563
10.42	The Universal House of Justice, Messages 1963 to 1986, p. 588
10.43	The Universal House of Justice, Messages 1963 to 1986, p. 685
10.44	Bahá'í International Community, 1995 Mar 03, The Prosperity of Humankind
10.45	Bahá'í International Community, 1999 Feb, Who is Writing the Future
10.46	Bahá'í International Community, 1999 Feb, Who is Writing the Future
10.47	Bahá'í International Community, 1999 Feb, Who is Writing the Future

Appendix: Sources and Bibliography 173

Chapter 11
11.1   Baha'u'llah, Tablets of Baha'u'llah, p. 22
11.2   Bahá'u'lláh, Gleanings from the Writings of Bahá'u'lláh, p. 325
11.3   Bahá'u'lláh, Gleanings from the Writings of Bahá'u'lláh, p. 10
11.4   Bahá'u'lláh, Gleanings from the Writings of Bahá'u'lláh, p. 11
11.5   Bahá'u'lláh, Gleanings from the Writings of Bahá'u'lláh, p. 136
11.6   Bahá'u'lláh, The Seven Valleys, p. 7
11.7   Bahá'u'lláh, Tablets of Bahá'u'lláh, p. 235
11.8   Bahá'u'lláh, Gleanings from the Writings of Bahá'u'lláh, p. 290
11.9   Bahá'u'lláh, The Kitáb-i-Iqan, p. 123
11.10 'Abdu'l-Bahá, Selections from the Writings of 'Abdu'l-Bahá, p. 29
11.11 'Abdu'l-Bahá, Selections from the Writings of 'Abdu'l-Bahá, p. 316
11.12 'Abdu'l-Bahá, Selections from the Writings of 'Abdu'l-Bahá, p. 319
11.13 'Abdu'l-Bahá, The Promulgation of Universal Peace, p. 452
11.14 Shoghi Effendi, The World Order of Bahá'u'lláh, p. 114
11.15 The Universal House of Justice, 1992 Dec 10, Issues Related to Study Compilation
11.16 The Universal House of Justice, 1992 Dec 10, Issues Related to Study Compilation
11.17 The Universal House of Justice, 1992 Nov 26, Second Message to World Congress

Chapter 12
12.1   Bahá'u'lláh, Gleanings from the Writings of Bahá'u'lláh, p. 65
12.2   Bahá'u'lláh, The Hidden Words, Arabic #55
12.3   Bahá'u'lláh, The Hidden Words, Persian #58
12.4   Bahá'u'lláh, Gleanings from the Writings of Bahá'u'lláh, p. 79
12.5   'Abdu'l-Bahá, The Promulgation of Universal Peace, p. 452
12.6   'Abdu'l-Bahá, The Promulgation of Universal Peace, p. 218
12.7   'Abdu'l-Bahá, The Promulgation of Universal Peace, p. 297
12.8   'Abdu'l-Bahá, The Promulgation of Universal Peace, p. 234
12.9   'Abdu'l-Bahá, The Promulgation of Universal Peace, p. 297
12.10 'Abdu'l-Bahá, The Promulgation of Universal Peace, p. 147
12.11 'Abdu'l-Bahá, The Promulgation of Universal Peace, p. 470
12.12 Shoghi Effendi, The World Order of Bahá'u'lláh, p. 60
12.13 The Universal House of Justice, 1992 Dec 10, Issues Related to Study Compilation

BIBLIOGRAPHY

Bahá'u'lláh. *The Seven Valleys*. Wilmette, Illinois, Bahá'í Publishing Trust: 1986 Edition
Bahá'u'lláh. *The Kitáb-i-Iqan*. Wilmette, Illinois, Bahá'í Publishing Trust: 1983 Edition
Bahá'u'lláh. *The Hidden Words*. Wilmette, Illinois, Bahá'í Publishing Trust: 2002 Edition
Bahá'u'lláh. *Tablets of Bahá'u'lláh*. Wilmette, Illinois: Bahá'í Publishing Trust, 1983 Edition
Bahá'u'lláh. *Gleanings from the Writings of Bahá'u'lláh*. Wilmette, Illinois: Bahá'í Publishing Trust, 1983 Edition
Bahá'u'lláh. *Prayers and Meditations by Bahá'u'lláh*. Wilmette, Illinois, Bahá'í Publishing Trust: 1987 Edition
Bahá'u'lláh. *The Proclamation of Bahá'u'lláh*. Wilmette, Illinois: Bahá'í Publishing Trust, 1967 Edition
Bahá'u'lláh. *Epistle to the Son of the Wolf*. Wilmette, Illinois: Bahá'í Publishing Trust, 1988 Edition
Bahá'u'lláh. *The Kitab-i-Aqdas*. Wilmette, Illinois: Bahá'í Publishing Trust, 1992 Edition
Bahá'u'lláh. *The Summons of the Lord of Hosts*. Haifa, Bahá'í World Centre, 2002 Edition

'Abdu'l-Bahá. *Selections from the Writings of 'Abdu'l-Bahá*. Haifa: Bahá'í World Centre, 1982 Edition
'Abdu'l-Bahá. *Tablets of the Divine Plan*. Wilmette, Illinois: Bahá'í Publishing Trust, 1993 Edition
'Abdu'l-Bahá. *The Promulgation of Universal Peace*. Wilmette, Illinois: Bahá'í Publishing Trust, 1982 Edition

'Abdu'l-Bahá. *Some Answered Questions*. Wilmette, Illinois: Bahá'í Publishing Trust, 1987 Edition
'Abdu'l-Bahá. *Paris Talks*. London: Bahá'í Publishing Trust, 1995
'Abdu'l-Bahá. *'Abdu'l-Bahá in London*. London: Bahá'í Publishing Trust, 1983
'Abdu'l-Bahá. *Secret of Divine Civilization*. London: Bahá'í Publishing Trust, 2007

Shoghi Effendi. *The Promised Day is Come*. Wilmette, Illinois: Bahá'í Publishing Trust, 1996 Edition
Shoghi Effendi. *The Advent of Divine Justice*. Wilmette, Illinois: Bahá'í Publishing Trust, 2003 Edition
Shoghi Effendi. *The World Order of Bahá'u'lláh*. Wilmette, Illinois: Bahá'í Publishing Trust, 1993 Edition
Shoghi Effendi. *Citadel of Faith*. Wilmette, Illinois: Bahá'í Publishing Trust, 2000 Edition
Shoghi Effendi. *God Passes By*. Wilmette, Illinois: Bahá'í Publishing Trust, 1974 Edition
Shoghi Effendi. *Dawn of a New Day*. New Delhi. Bahá'í Publishing Trust, 1974 Edition
Shoghi Effendi. *Summary Statement - 1947, Special UN Committee on Palestine*. Haifa, Bahá'í World Centre

The Universal House of Justice, *The Promise of World Peace*, Haifa, 1985
The Universal House of Justice, *Wellspring of Guidance, Messages 1963 to 1986*. Wilmette, Illinois: Bahá'í Publishing Trust, 1970 Edition
The *Universal House of Justice, Issues Related to Study Compilation*. Haifa: 1992 Dec 10.

Bahá'í International Community, 1995 Jan 10, *Promoting Religious Tolerance*
Bahá'í International Community, 1988 Feb 17, *Eliminating Religious Intolerance*
Bahá'í International Community. 1987 *The Bahá'í Statement on Nature*
Bahá'í International Community. 1988 Aug 01, *Rights of Indigenous Populations*
Bahá'í International Community. 1995 Mar 03, *The Prosperity of Humankind*
Bahá'í International Community. 1999 Feb, *Who is Writing the Future*

The Compilation of Compilations vol. I & vol II. Prepared by the Research Department of the Universal House of Justice. Maryborough, Victoria: Bahá'í Publications Australia, 1991
Lights of Guidance. Compiled by Helen Hornby. New Delhi. Bahá'í Publishing Trust, 1994 Edition

The copyright of this text in no way modifies the copyright status of the above publications.

WhyUnite?
because your journey matters to the world.

We hope you have enjoyed this WhyUnite? book. We are committed to providing quality introductory materials for the Bahá'í Faith across all mediums. To learn more about our products, find recommendations for further reading, and connect with more Bahá'ís, please visit: http://www.whyunite.com

www.ingramcontent.com/pod-product-compliance
Lightning Source LLC
Chambersburg PA
CBHW020856090426
42736CB00008B/396